Hell on Earth:
Dancing with the Elites & Running with the Junkyard Dogs

by

Craig Weaver

DORRANCE PUBLISHING CO
EST. 1920
PITTSBURGH, PENNSYLVANIA 15238

The contents of this work, including, but not limited to, the accuracy of events, people, and places depicted; opinions expressed; permission to use previously published materials included; and any advice given or actions advocated are solely the responsibility of the author, who assumes all liability for said work and indemnifies the publisher against any claims stemming from publication of the work.

All Rights Reserved
Copyright © 2022 by Craig Weaver

No part of this book may be reproduced or transmitted, downloaded, distributed, reverse engineered, or stored in or introduced into any information storage and retrieval system, in any form or by any means, including photocopying and recording, whether electronic or mechanical, now known or hereinafter invented without permission in writing from the publisher.

Dorrance Publishing Co
585 Alpha Drive
Pittsburgh, PA 15238
Visit our website at *www.dorrancebookstore.com*

ISBN: 979-8-8852-7217-9
eISBN: 979-8-8852-7673-3

Table of Contents

Preface 1
Introduction 9
Chapter 1: THE PERFECT STORM 11
Chapter 2: MY BUSINESS SNOWBALLS
           AND TURNS INTO AN EMPIRE 21
Chapter 3: Consequences of Opioids:
           "HERE COMES DA JUDGE" 25
Chapter 4: WORK RELEASE: UNLEASH
           THE BUSINESSMAN 31
Chapter 5: LIFE ON THE LAMB: GO WEST YOUNG MAN . . .35
Chapter 6: Arrested in Tucson:
           TIME TO DO THE IMPOSSIBLE 45
Chapter 7: NO WAY OUT! TRAPPED IN
           MY HELL ON EARTH 63
Chapter 8: ENTER: HEROIN - NO MORE MAINTAINING . . .85
Chapter 9: NO MORE REALITY: I AM ANIMAL 93
Chapter 10: Everything must go:
            MONEY AND SUCCESS TURN EVIL 119
Chapter 11: TOTAL INSANITY: DEATH SOUNDS
            DAMN GOOD 125
Chapter 12: BACK FROM HELL: A NEW LIFE 131

ACKNOWLEGEMENTS

I'm alive! I'm healthy! My self esteem has returned! To save myself from opioid addiction, I threw away a fortune! My guilt is gone and I have forgiven myself! Due to a combination of uncontrollable traumatic situations during my youth, I spent three decades battling this insidious disease of opioid addiction, an obsessive compulsive disorder, a horrific football injury and a drug addicted doctor. It was the perfect storm! Today after twelve years clean, I hold my head high! I help other sick and suffering addicts. I live life with passion . Faith- hope - hard work- throw in some love and there is freedom from addiction!

My deepest thanks and gratitude to:

Barb Petney, Three years ago I painted her house.
Curiosity got the best of her and she transposed my book
from a $25.00 tape recorder to paper! Today we are amazing friends!

Craig 1 and Dr. Sue Wicker, Bought food off me for twenty years! They watched my transition! God Bless both of them for they believed in me and without their backing I would not have a book!

Archie Hamer, Real Estate agent and my landlord
allowed me to pretend I was a carpenter and backed me 100%!

Stay tuned! I'm sure the adventure will continue.

PREFACE

I am lying on a gurney in the emergency room at the hospital in Indiana, Pennsylvania, slipping in and out of consciousness. All I could remember is how bright those damn fluorescent lights were -and the pain. I will never forget that pain. Why did I keep waking up? I just wanted to be put out of my misery so fucking bad.

Then I see this disheveled looking old haggard man staring down at me. He looked like a bum- hair growing everywhere, a three-day growth on his face. He stunk. He actually reeked of sweat. I remember that. As much pain as I was in, that I remember.

"I'm your doctor James P. Berkeley. Your leg is a mess, son. Your left femur is busted in half above the kneecap. You're in trouble. You're going to be here for a long time. You see this break is so close to the kneecap I can't pin it back together and then cast it."

Oh my God, what the hell is going on! I thought to myself. *I must be dead. In hell.*

Then this disgusting smelly doctor said, "We're going to have to put your leg in traction and try to pull that bone together."

What! How long? I will never forget these next words out of the doctor's mouth.

He bends over and whispers, "The pain will be excruciating; you're going to have twenty pounds of weight pulling on your broken bone constantly but I'm going to make sure you do not feel a damn thing. In fact, you are going to enjoy your stay with us."

I swear I think I started balling like a little kid. I'm in a fucking twilight zone. Is this true? Is this happening?

OK back to reality. That afternoon I was playing a yearly tackle football game with my fraternity Phi Kappa Si at Indiana University of Pennsylvania.

We split into two teams. I was playing defense at the time. I was a linebacker. Now you would think this would be a friendly game between brothers of the fraternity. No. Dissention abounded. The other linebacker beside me was a mortal enemy of the offensive running back. They could not stand each other.

Well, the running back 250 lbs., no fat- very athletic, decides to physically hurt my teammate. I mean he wanted to hurt him bad. So full speed ahead comes the halfback. My teammate moves out of the way leaving me exposed to this maniac. Now picture a 250 lb. locomotive flying thru the air hitting my femur with the small of his back in mid-flight.

Crack! They say the sound could be heard 100 yards away. I was down. The few people around me were puking at the sight of my contorted leg- it was shaped like a "V" right above the knee. The next thing I remember is waking up in the emergency room and screaming in pain, staring at this creepy Dr. Berkeley saying really weird shit to me.

Now here is where the twists and turns start happening...

Dr. Berkeley was the chief bone specialist during the Vietnam War in the field. And even though it was years later, this doctor was a total drug addict, addicted to opioids. He was trying to maintain, and I was thrown into his world against my will. So, at nineteen years old, three months into this traction, Dr. Berkeley said I was going to be crippled, to a certain degree; unchartered territory.

The hospital stay was out of the ordinary. I was high.

I was stoned. A shot of morphine every four hours. Pain pills in between for quote -breakthrough pain - muscle relaxers, Valium, sleeping pills. But I waited for that shot of morphine every day, every hour, every second. The medical records show the number of opioids I was given would have had five elephants addicted.

For three months I had to lay flat on my back with a twenty-pound weight pulling on my leg from the bottom of the bed! If I even moved my leg, a jolt of pain would shoot through my body like a shot of powerful electricity! I took everything I was given and this new feeling of euphoria would flow thru my head.

Once you get over the nausea, lightheadedness, and a few other small side effects of the opioids, your endorphins can receive higher doses! This in turn takes you to a new place you've never been before! A warmth comes over you. Everything is OK.

My personality would change to where I loved talking to people. I joked around with everyone! It's a wonderful place to be for a while. I was also taking Valium and muscle relaxers, so I had a cocktail that really just made everything around me seem amazing! Not a care in the world! A brother in the fraternity brought me in a little one hit bong. It fit nicely in the drawer beside me. The nurse and I became close friends and she would bring me in pot every couple of days. So along with my six shots of morphine and twenty-seven pills per day I was smoking pot.

By the way, this nurse was also very athletic and could hang off the traction bar and straddle me. At nineteen years old I was like a loaded weapon.

So she was nursing me back to health.

When I look back-WOW! Everything was being catered to me. I had a TV with Pong set up on it! Remember the first one. The dot travels back and forth on the screen and each side had a bar to hit it back and forth.

I had all the pot I wanted. I was getting laid by a beautiful nurse and I was constantly in the euphoric state. I guess the road to hell is not only paved with good intentions; it has some awesome stops on the way.

The doctor gave me a private room and told the staff I was allowed visitors any time. I swear my room was the place to go. Weekends were filled up! People slept over because they were too stoned to go home. I shared!

OK, so at the tender age of nineteen after two semesters at the Indiana University of Pennsylvania I'm thrown into a situation that little did I know would change my entire life. I left that hospital after three months, a full-fledged opioid drug addict.

It was the late 1970s. Not much was known about drug addiction back then. There was Betty Ford Clinic and then there was Gateway Rehab. outside of Pittsburgh. This event sent me spiraling into a world of unbelievable suffering, pain associated with people and places I never knew existed... disgusting, pure darkness, gloom, doom. People eventually lose everything that is good, their soul, their mind, and their ability to love.

You cannot love anything but the pills that keep you functioning. We travel down a road that only leads to darkness and despair. We are society's freaks.

The things I did, the places I ended up were utterly sick and twisted. Me, a highly intelligent athlete, ready to take on life. Be the American dream.

I had it in the palm of my hands. Then one football injury with the wrong doctor and other circumstances led to what I call the perfect storm. Oh my God I would have to live two lives in one. I would go to "DANCE WITH THE ELITES AND RUN WITH THE JUNKYARD DOGS." This would be my life.

I had to live with a horrific secret that would turn into "HELL ON EARTH."

Come with me into this world. Let me show you the real horrors of opioid addiction never told like this before. I will totally go into what really happens how you really feel -the ins and outs, the never-ending despair and pain, the suffering- the sheer animalistic behavior that can consume anyone who enters into this world. There is evil all around. This disease does not want you in a rehab. It does not want you in jail.

This evil insidious disease -wants you dead!

As I sit here with over nine years clean, I thank God I made it. I was and still am blessed. I should by all rights be dead. I'm not! I am more alive now than all the years I spent sick and suffering with this disease. Life is so precious. Please, this is a must read! I love opening my eyes every morning and feeling at peace with the world! I beat it! I don't care how many years you've been a slave to addiction, you can learn to love life again!

You have to make a solid decision to want to be clean! You must reach deeper down into your heart and soul than you ever have and Just Let Go! TIME is key. For sixty to ninety days, if you stop taking your drugs of choice; or anything addictive, you will be free! Get a higher power, your choice. Surround yourself with good, clean people who want to help no matter how bad the pain gets! Stay tough! I promise you, in sixty to ninety days, you will open your eyes one morning and actually feel a new sense of elation! A new and real high for life will overcome you. There's a big beautiful world out there; grab onto it and don't let go.

Thank the Lord again I am one of a few people who made it out. I have over nine years clean and I love waking up every morning. So like I said- come with me. But buckle up. It is a ride straight down to the depths of HELL ON EARTH.

HELL ON EARTH:
Dancing with the Elites & Running with the Junkyard Dogs

by

Craig Weaver

INTRODUCTION

My name is Craig Weaver.

I was caught in the perfect storm. During the early eighties opioid addiction took me by surprise. It all started with a busted femur while playing a fraternity football game at IUP.

I was placed in traction with a twenty-pound weight pulling my bone back together for three months! Combine the excruciating pain with a doctor from the Vietnam War who was also an opioid addict FROM the war. Not only did the massive influx of opioids alter the chemical makeup of my brain, but enter the final piece of the puzzle- a very dysfunctional childhood. The massive doses of opioids gave me a storage room to hold the forbidden and painful secrets of my childhood.

I found my salvation! The high from opioids freed my mind from all the torment and suffering that plagued me every second, of every minute, of every day. Little did I know, my lifelong conundrum was born. The perfect storm arrived. Yes, the opiates freed me from my demons but would also take me through three decades of hell on earth! My journey took me to the deepest, darkest places where no one should go. At the same time my endorphins were dancing among the elites of society, I would be forced to run and live with the junkyard dogs! Two lives in one.

Come with me. Let me take you through my world where I would change hell into heaven leading me down the longer path turning heaven into HELL ON EARTH!

BUCKLE UP!

CHAPTER 1
THE PERFECT STORM

When I say my opioid addiction started the perfect storm, we have to go back to my childhood. Follow me through this; our youth and our upbringing play a massive role in addiction. Our early years growing up are key.

Addiction usually stems from some major dysfunctionality either from social injustices as a child or pain, injuries and things that you sustain while being a kid that are with you and you cannot get out of your mind. These traumatic events or injuries bother you every minute of every hour of every day.

So let's go. Start with my family. I come from a really good gene pool. My uncle Eddie worked on the lunar module that landed on the moon! He worked for Lockheed Martin as an aerospace engineer. He actually quit for a while and moved back here to this area to become a partner in my home delivery steak and seafood business. We found out he wasn't a salesman so after two years he went back to being a "spaceman." My uncle Kenny was the chief postal inspector of the United States. It was like the FBI of the postal system. His two main cases were the Unabomber and the anthrax scare. He was on the national news quite a bit. My third uncle was the assistant superintendent of Conrail out of Clearfield, Pennsylvania.

My father moved up in supervision with the railroad. He was the superintendent of Newark, New Jersey and New York City and basically made it to the ranks of taking care of the eastern coast. This is the main part of the railroad that supplies the whole eastern coast with goods. Everyone on my mother's side became doctors, lawyers, government workers. So basically, I come from good stock.

But I came from a major dysfunctional family. My father was a railroader in a little town of Cresson, Pennsylvania. He and my mother got married way before they should have. Dad was eighteen and Mom was seventeen. Dad would work his eight-hour shift then go with his railroad buddies and get drunk every day before he would come home. Mom didn't drink and Dad had a violent temper. And the two of them would fight constantly. I was the oldest out of three. I remember everything.

Dad would go into these rages. Me, my little sister and my little brother watched everything happen. And believe you me you do not forget a thing. Not a day went by without yelling, shouting or other altercations. All three of us kids lived in total fear of Dad. Dad was like this huge powerful giant yelling at Mom. She came to really despise him. This was our big secret, our family secret. Nobody knew this. To the outside world we were the perfect middle class family unit. This is how it went for years; my father would work from seven in the morning until 3 o'clock in the afternoon. He would stop at the bar. My mother, myself and my siblings would sit on the couch to see if he was coming straight home from work.

Now if he was home a little after three then everything was ok. That means Dad was not drinking, which very seldomly happened. When 3:45 came and went, we would start warning mom- "don't start a fight, don't pick, just be quiet, mom." We all sat there trembling. Dad would come home between five and six and would always start on our mother. He was just being a prick and picking on her trying to start a fight. He would say anything to make her talk back. Finally, she did and a fight would ensue. Then my father would lose it. At times mom would run into the bathroom with Dad running after her slamming the door. Bang! Smash! Us kids were outside screaming at the top of our lungs. "Stop Dad! Stop! Don't hurt mom!" Dad would run out of the house slamming the door and mom would come out of the bathroom crying.

You see that was my father's excuse to go back out with his crazy friends, get drunk and raise hell. My father's nickname was "Bear" and he owned that name. His temper was that of a bear. He would be fine. Then one wrong word or the smallest negative thing would send him into an outburst or a rage anywhere, anytime. I called this his adult temper tantrums. My father could have used some therapy, but back in the sixties you just didn't do that. He was just an angry man! He always told me about my grandfather's class ring banging off the back of his head and how bad it hurt. I guess Grandpap always smacked my dad with his ring and dad remembered that. So all three of us kids grew up to hate and love our father. It's one of those things that many people deal with and it's very traumatic. I would wait up until two or three in the morning to make sure my father would come home. He would go to bed with my mother and pass out. I had to make sure mom was ok. So many nights I could hear huge fights in the bedroom. Many times, mom would run into my room and use me as a shield to protect her. Now this is from the age of twelve on.

All through school we all grew up so insecure and frightened about what's going to happen in our home. What's going to happen tonight? Will we have any peace? Will we have any serenity? Not a day went by without a huge altercation. I'm damaged about that even to this day, so was my sister and my brother. This was one of my three dysfunctionalities as a youth.

As children we love and look up to both parents. Sometimes they don't realize their confrontations affect us kids! Every day we would worry; we would pray for a good evening. When they would get into these battles, it really affected us worse than they will ever know. We all experienced certain insecurities from those dark days.

Now if that isn't bad enough here comes the second dysfunctionality. At five years old I went to the neighbors to pet their dog, a big Dalmatian shepherd. I liked the dog and went over a lot. One day I was ready to pet him. They had just finished dinner and threw out a bunch of chicken bones for him to eat. As I went to pet him, he lunged at me and ripped the entire right side of my face off. It took 258 stitches later that night to try to put my face back together. After that I had to have eight operations every two years when my face would grow a little bit. Starting grade school, I had a huge scar on the right side of my face. I mean huge! All I will say is kids are brutal. And I was massively paranoid.

OK now, last but not least I inherited cystic acne from my mother. She had it bad. From the age of thirteen on, my face, neck, and shoulders had big deep sores all over, not pimples – big deep sores!

They hurt so bad and I was always trying to pop them or fix them. I always had three or four on my face. And when one would go away another one would come. I wrestled in high school and had to wear three t-shirts due to the acne breaking open during the match. At the end of every match there were bloodstains all over my shirts. I was so paranoid about that.

Let's just say it straight. Cystic acne is nothing but sores filled with pus that open. It's very painful. And people don't realize what it will do to you and what it puts you through mentally- to try to act normal with these sores all over your face, especially when you're growing through your adolescent years. All my friends were jocks like me and they would get the nice girls. Due to the cystic acne, I had a harder time trying to fit in and find the right girl. Cystic acne is something that you think about constantly. It would cause me to continuously go to the bathroom while at school to see how everything looked. This caused me to hate mirrors.

OK, let's throw all these together...

Number 1 – I was insecure and worried all day about my father and my life at home. I lived in fear at home, scared to death about what each night would bring.

Number 2- a gigantic scar on the right side of my face- ear to mouth, thick and wide.

Number 3- cystic acne. Let's call it what it really is. Huge pus-filled sores that could and would break open at any time causing a disgusting mess.

Now let me tell you exactly what I went through mentally every second of every minute of every hour of every fucking day. All these major childhood disasters would flood my thoughts. I could not concentrate or enjoy what was going on at the time. I was always thinking how I looked, what was going to happen when I got home. So anything I found that would give me a break or take my mind off of these, I would obsess in. For some reason acting out externalizing my energy instead of inwardly – like speaking in front of the whole class or having everyone's attention. For some reason, it blocked my thoughts from internalizing. It seemed like the larger the crowd the more comfortable I was talking and being myself. I was actually deemed the class clown. This in turn gave me one hell of a personality. Shooting pool was another escape. I would play pool by myself for hours upon hours upon hours. I actually turned semi-pro and was amazing by the age of nineteen. I mean I could've been so good. So many stories about that.

So, this is how my OCD started- obsessive compulsive disorder. Put this together with my hospital and doctor experience at the age of nineteen.

When I walked out of that hospital, my life would be changed forever. It was like the coming together of the perfect storm. Those opioids I was taking, the drugs I became addicted to- they would give me freedom I never had. They would enable me to shove all my problems back in the back of my brain. And I would forget about everything. Yes, self-medicating with opioids was my salvation. I did not have a fucking chance when I left that hospital.

You see, not only did I spend three months in traction, I left the hospital with a full length cast up to my hip. This cast stayed on for a year and a half. Dr, Berkeley kept the flow of opioids coming. I made a half-assed attempt to go back to school with a full-length cast and my new disease. I was loved at the fraternity house but all I did was party. I was a mess! School had to end and it did. Get ready for this.

One night I was out at a bar drinking and talking to this attractive girl. I ended up taking her back to the fraternity house and we had sex. I later found out she was the girlfriend of the head Animal biker gang member who was coming after me to kill me. I was lifted from this fate by my uncle coming to pick me up due to my little brother's death.

My little brother was killed at age of fourteen. I was in college. Dad quit Supervision due to his temper! He could not handle the stress-filled job, so he decided to move the family back to Blue Knob, Pennsylvania and go back to being a tower operator. My little brother Chris was so bored being in the country, so Dad promised to get him a four-wheeler! Well, every day Dad would tell Chris, "As soon as I get home from work, I'll grab you and we'll go get a four-wheeler." Day after day Dad never showed up! Always stopping at the bars! One day Chris was waiting for him and the neighbor just got his driver's license.

"Come on Chris, let's go for a ride!"

Chris got tired of waiting for Dad and jumped in his car! 120 miles an hour-they crashed into a tree.

Chris broke his neck and died. My father felt so guilty for not being there for Chris and not being able to protect him. This wrecked my father. Guilt was horrendous! He quit drinking for a year. I miss my brother so bad!

Alright let's go. I became an opioid addict at the age of nineteen. That was around 1978, 1979. Very little was known about addiction. So we had an intelligent good-looking overachiever who had to quit college but still ready to tackle the world. Only I had a monkey on my back. I had a disease. I had no clue how dangerous this was. All I knew is that when I took opioids I forgot about my problems and that was fine with me. Little did I know I was a slave to a deadly disease that I would have to keep hidden from the world. Leaving the hospital, I did not realize how much it would change my life, how I would be a completely different person. The life that I once knew was gone!

Keep reading and I guarantee so much twisting and turning in my life with living two lives in one. This disease is insidious and only gets worse.

When I left the hospital, I had to wear the cast for a year and a half.

For that year and a half, I was given unlimited scripts of Percocet, Valium and some other very strong pain medications. So one day I decided to go and visit my friends at the University of Pittsburgh. I had just gotten my cast off. I was supposed to be crippled. My bone only healed 80%. In other words, there was a 20% angle. I worked day after day learning how to walk correctly; one foot this way, the other foot this way. I beat it. I don't have a limp. So that was a good thing. But I needed to start a life. College was no more. Money ran out and I couldn't work. So I was visiting my friends at the University of Pittsburgh and saw an ad in the paper. I needed a vehicle. It was a steak and seafood delivery service door to door and it advertised "a vehicle will be provided for you".

I said, "Okay... I can kill two birds with one stone. I can get a vehicle and I can go out and make some money."

I knew I was a good salesman. And I could bullshit like nobody else.

So I went and got the job. This would alter my life. To this day I am still known as "The Meat Man." I started this home delivery steak and seafood business with a company called Anchors Away in Pittsburgh. I had a vehicle but I was charged $18 a day for this vehicle so it wasn't free. I started a territory. I was damn good. Dr. Berkeley became a customer of mine right away. He was still supplying me with opioids and I started to supply him with food. I had no idea how badly I was addicted, how dangerous this disease was. I was in my early twenties by now full of energy and life. I kicked ass and became their best salesman.

I had customers everywhere from Oakland, Maryland, Pittsburgh, Pennsylvania, Clearfield, PA, Philipsburg, PA, State College, Lewistown, Harrisburg…And what I did was wrote down their names and phone numbers and made it a monthly thing. Every customer I got, I would put them on a calling list. And I would come to their house with a truckload of steaks, shrimp and lobster tails, crabcakes all in $30-$40 boxes. I would take orders and deliver them. And I found out that when you called people in advance and get orders from them, you could set up a system. And it worked beautifully.

Now as my business grew, I realized I was paying too much for the product.

So, I went out and found my own distributors. I found two really good whole sale distributors. After a few years I had one hell of a business!

But as my business grew, as the stress grew, my addiction grew. I was addicted to about six to eight Percocet per day at this time. I was maintaining which you can do for a while. Besides Dr. Berkeley, I started finding other places to get more pills. You always run out. They say for all addicts, "one pill is too many and a thousand is not enough".

So I started finding other sources, other people. I started going into back alleys of towns. I would just find out where the pills were. And believe me back in those days you could find the inner circles where these addicts ran. And I was good at that also.

I made a delivery to Dr. Berkeley once a month until- get ready for this-a huge twist. Buckle up!

One day I stopped by Dr. Berkeley's office for a food order. He would check the items off, give me a check. Then I would drive to his "slum mansion" as I called it. It was a mansion but the place was a mess. It was just unattended to. He had a daughter and two sons that were stoned all the time either uppers or downers. And they were a mess every time I went there. Then there was his wife whom I met one time from hearing screams on the second floor in bed.

The daughter said, "oh, that's my mom, she needs her morphine."

I said, "what?

All I heard was, "Where's my morphine? Dammit! You better call your father and get him home!"

Well, the daughter took me upstairs. Here's this disheveled old lady lying in bed. She couldn't weigh more than 80 lbs. just yelling and screaming that she needs her morphine. I felt so bad for her. So one day I was there. She's screaming for her morphine. It was the twilight zone. I couldn't wait to leave their place. But I got such big orders and we had a deal where we traded for pain pills. Therefore I had to continue my association with Dr. Berkeley. We kind of made a deal to take care of each other. So anyway Dr. Berkeley comes home early that day. And I'm still there. He goes upstairs and gives his wife her daily shot. All of a sudden everything got quiet. This is twenty minutes later.

The daughter says, "Something's wrong. Mom usually comes down or keeps yelling or feels better. We haven't heard from her." The daughter goes upstairs and I hear this blood curdling scream. "Mom's dead! Mom's dead!"

Yes, she overdosed and she died. Doc gave her a tad too much. I hightailed it out of there and never returned. From what I hear, Dr. Berkeley got a four-year sentence for involuntary manslaughter. He lost his license forever. And that was the best thing that could've happened. He had so many patients addicted. He was ruining so many lives. His kids went to rehabs the last I heard. Hell on earth ladies and gentlemen, hell on earth.

Now that's when I had to start hunting for my own opioids. I sold food to so many doctors who would oblige. Back then it was easy. They wanted to do something they thought was nice for you. Not even the doctors knew how deadly this opioid addiction was yet. "What do you need son? Here, here's thirty Percocet. This will help. Just give me some nice filet mignon or lobster tails." It worked too well. To furnish my habit I also had to meet people around all these towns where you don't want to go. You search them out. You find out where they live. You sell some food to them. But basically, you're just starting to make your "connections". It was almost another business. Soon with all the towns I sold food in, I had tons of pill buddies.

It was like a club. Everyone knew what everyone wanted. And whoever had it at the time would sell them to each other. We'd share. We'd try to keep everybody well back in those days. It was a secret little cult. And every town has one and they're growing. They're getting worse. Looking back, that was my indoctrination into the secret world of opioid addiction. I was in eight towns every four weeks.

So, therein lies the beginning of my secret double life.

CHAPTER 2
MY BUSINESS SNOWBALLS AND TURNS INTO AN EMPIRE

A few years go by and my business snowballs. It actually grew bigger than I ever thought. I can honestly remember selling to the wealthiest people and the middle class in every single town and I was known as "The Meat Man". To this day I'm still known as "The Meat Man". I probably had over 800 customers by then. I put them all on a calling list and would get their orders before I went. It was working beautifully. I then put three other trucks out on the road. I had three of my best friends who were all good salesmen working for me. They went out started their own territories. I taught them everything I knew. They were good salesmen. My friends all got their own territories by going out and hustling.

We were in our early twenties so we were partying also. We would all go to a town or city together like say for example, Harrisburg. We would go down sell food all day and meet at a nightclub. We would party all-night, pick-up women. And who the hell knew where we would end up the next morning.

We couldn't find one of our guys one morning, searched everywhere. We were getting worried. We were parked in back of a nightclub and we see this body come crawling out of a trash bin. He passed out in a trash container and that's where he slept. It wasn't a good night for him. These were crazy times. I was young and healthy enough to maintain my addiction and drink all night with the boys. We sold a ton of food during those days.

I just never cared enough about saving money or investing money because it came too easy.

I think due to my youth due to all I went through with my family, my scar, my acne, everything! – I only cared about the day, the present. I can remember thinking I just want to have a good day and night. I would make reward systems where I would work hard all day and when the night came -be with a woman and party- and pay my bills. That's how I lived. I never ever thought of the future.

I couldn't keep all the boys organized enough over a few years due to the partying and the crazy lifestyle we led. My addiction played a big role in that also. So they sooner or later found other jobs- salesmen jobs. They were all good guys and they all had good lives. That was a crazy good time in my life, my early twenties. I was traveling with my best buddies, we tore up, made a lot of money. Good years.

When they left, I inherited all their customers. So add all three of their customer bases to my customer base. My business just went off the rails. It was amazing! I would sell to fifteen or twenty houses in a day and go home and make phone calls for the next day and do it again. If I needed more money in a day, I'd just make a few more phone calls. There were days I'd clear $400, some days $600, some days $1,000. But the work was hard. It was so hard. Spending hours in the morning getting the food from different distributors, taking it to my warehouse, packing it -then by 11 in the morning I would take off and sell to State College, Clearfield, Pittsburgh. And I had to logisticize all my stops. Twenty stops in a day and I did it. Wow! How did I do that?

Oh, here comes another twist. Right around twenty-five years old, I made a friend.

I was selling to the owner of Precious Metals and Diamonds in Johnstown, Pennsylvania- David. He was taking off in jewelry, one of the biggest distributors on the eastern sea coast. Once he showed me the markup in 14K gold and necklaces, I could not believe it. So I made a $1,000 gold purchase and started taking a little display to my food customers. Well, that was the beginning of my claim to fame. I went from taking a small jewelry display with my food to about $60,000 worth of jewelry paid for within a year. My wealthy customers would order these huge tennis bracelets and big 3K diamonds. It was the hit. The owner of Precious Metals and Diamonds would let me take out anything I wanted to show these people. Like if a doctor's wife wanted to look at three huge diamonds., he would let me take three huge diamonds out on an article of consignment. And I would sell her the ones she liked and just take the others back. Boy did that come into use later on. We became very tight. The owner and me were working together amazingly. I would take so much stuff out on consignment but at same time building up my own display, buying more and more and paying it off in a couple of months. After a while he gave me a $100,000 credit limit. I was growing faster than I ever imagined with jewelry. Then I decided to put up a jewelry store. My parents decided to buy in and go in halves with me. This was the beginning of my jewelry empire along with my steak and seafood business.

Now at the same time, I would have to sneak off during the day and see my pill buddies. I would sneak down in the back streets of Altoona, Clearfield, Philipsburg... I knew people everywhere. And I would end up partying with them. I would end up staying with them. And I was getting to know these people. I was living two lives in one. And the sad thing is both were growing. My disease was alive and well. I was getting more and more addicted. And it seems the more stress you have, the more anxiety you have by running two businesses; your addiction feeds off that. You become immune to just a few pills. You need more and more and more.

And it was only my youth and I think from being an athlete I was in shape. And that gave me the ability to tackle both of these.

Then I started home jewelry parties. I would go to these rich people and these wives always had friends everywhere – they're cliques. I would offer the owner of a house-a customer, 10% of every jewelry sale at her party. "Just invite as many people as you can ten, twenty, thirty. I'll supply the wine. You want to get me drunk." And these ladies loved it. And what spurred them on was by that time I probably had a $60,000-$80,000 display. But then with my consignment deal with David, I would take out another $100,000 worth and take it to the jewelry party. These shows started kicking butt. I mean everyone wanted to have one. I was selling $5,000, $6,000, $8,000 worth at each show. Then I'd return the jewelry that was on consignment, buy a few nice pieces to upgrade my stock. And it was growing faster than I could ever imagine. Then I'd take menus to the jewelry parties. They would order food! So I'd get new food customers, sell a ton of jewelry, get drunk, have fun. And that's how those grew. Oh my God, these rich people -they try to outdo each other. The hostess of the party was making $600...$900 just to have one. Plus, it was a good experience for her to show off to her friends. "Look what I have in my house!" This was all about the cliques, all about the money, all about the fame.

Everyone in all my towns started loving jewelry parties. The store was doing good and it was running on its own. So my jewelry display was growing. My food business was doing great. All my towns were building.

But that monkey on my back was getting restless. I was becoming wealthy and I really didn't care. I had no idea what was going on. I just lived from day to day. My business was accelerating, snowballing. The two types of items I was selling just seemed to go together so well- filet mignons, lobster tails, shrimp and diamonds, rings, necklaces.

But I still had that secret world of "hell on earth" – that I hid from all these people. Oh, I had bad days. I had days where I would run out, couldn't find any pills. And I would be so sick. I would just wonder, "What the hell was going on? How could I ever get out of this?" I was living in two parallel universes. Now here's where it gets real, ladies and gentlemen. When you're an addict, you always brush up with the law. You always have your run-ins because you have to lie, cheat and steal to get what you need just to stay well. Forget about getting high anymore. You don't get high once you are a full-fledged addict. You just try to get well. Maybe you feel great for an hour or two. It gave you a jolt. But as far as feeling great all day, forget it.

You have to keep taking more and more.

CHAPTER 3

Consequences of Opioids –
"HERE COMES DA JUDGE"

Now I'm going to tell you about my first dance with trouble- the law. This can't be made up. I was around twenty-seven. I had eight good solid areas where I could go to a town and deliver $1,500 worth of food in a day and another $1,000-$2,000 in jewelry. Everything was going well except my disease. I was trapped. Opioids were now a part of my life, like alcohol to an alcoholic!

I was living day to day. Some days I'd feel like crap. Some days I would score a lot of pills and feel good. In Deep Creek Lake, Oakland, Maryland I had my wealthiest clients of all. It's about two hours from Altoona and all these families owned coal companies. They would buy $600 -$800 worth of food and then anything they wanted in jewelry. I can sincerely remember the times I would load up the truck with $3,000 worth of food, take down tons of jewelry, come back with no food and $10,000 in my pocket. I'm sitting here shaking my head as I write this. The money I was earning was incredible!

Before I go on, I must explain something about all the money I was making.

Growing up, it seemed like anytime a huge problem would arise, mom and dad would always have money to deal with it. We never had to worry about money! Dad had a pretty good job on the railroad as a tower operator and mom had a few businesses. At first, she was a hair stylist and after that she started a clothing store. She had two stores in a couple of towns! They also took my grandmother in and mom was power of attorney over her. "Gram" had a pretty nice chunk saved up. Money was never an issue.

Then when I started my businesses, I was making money hand over fist, a lot of it. I had absolutely no business skills. So here's what I would do. Instead of investing my extra cash flow or even saving it, I started getting obsessed about buying gold and diamonds. My OCD kicked in; I was making buys of thirty to forty thousand and paying them off in three months! I had this plan of acquiring massive amounts of jewelry to use for my future. But with my opioid addiction it would come to be "all for nothing." So sad!

Well, let's get back to Deep Creek. I met a girl down there. She was beautiful. She was hot. She was coming on to me. She would party at night. I would always get a motel room and we would party together. I was struck by her. We met a few times. But I never had sex with her. I wanted to but just never crossed that threshold. Well, I get a phone call one day.

"Craig," she says, "We are having a cocaine party down here in Oakland, Maryland. My distributor got in trouble and couldn't deliver an ounce of cocaine. Can you help me, please?"

Well, I knew cocaine distributors. She says, "If you bring me down an ounce of cocaine and save my party, you can stay here with me overnight. And I will make sure you are rewarded all night long." Now I remember it like yesterday. This girl is going to give me one hell of a night. That is all I thought about. I could care less about the cocaine. I didn't do cocaine. I was an opioid addict. But I knew people that had it and I could sure as hell get it for her. I wasn't cautious. I wasn't afraid. I wasn't leery. I knew nothing about the law. I had never been in trouble with the law, so I had no fear. No red flags showed up. I called and got an ounce of cocaine. Two of my friends stopped in on a Saturday night and I told them about the party in Maryland and they decided to go with me. I swear I never mentioned the cocaine. We just wanted to have fun. I just wanted the girl!

Here's where things get real. We were driving to Oakland with the ounce of cocaine hidden in my trunk singing Elvis Presley songs, and not a care in the world. I was to meet her in the parking lot of a Holiday Inn and give her the package. Then we would all head into the party together. I was going to get two rooms, one for my friends and one for the girl and me. We were so fired up. We got out of the car and gave a rendition of "Blue Suede Shoes" in the parking lot, dancing and singing at the top of our lungs, all three of us. I saw the girl coming out of her car. She was laughing. She comes over and hands me the $1,200. I give her the cocaine package.

And then all hell breaks loose! Cops, dogs, shotguns, pistols, handcuffs everywhere.

The sheriff in charge grabs me and says, "Drugs are illegal in this town, boy."

That was his big line. I wonder how long it took him to come up with that one. He probably saw it in a movie.

Oh my God, the next thing I know we are in the Garrett County Jail. Everyone's being interrogated. Here we go, my life's over. It took our families seven days to figure out what was going on and come down. We went to the bail hearing in front of Judge Taylor. Now the things you are about to read cannot be made up. Remember, crazy twists and turns. This girl's boyfriend got busted in Oakland. She was trying to help him get out of trouble by making some busts for him by "snitching." It was all a setup. Jack Slat of Oakland, Maryland is his name and Kathy is his girl. They told the district attorney that I was this huge drug dealer from Pennsylvania and I had them chomping at the bit. They thought I was Al Capone. You see an ounce of cocaine is the largest bust ever in this small town. I am done. The DA would not budge off of a twenty-year sentence.

Now as fate would have it, I was not a drug dealer. I was an opioid addict. I was selling food and jewelry to Oakland, Maryland.

Judge Taylor, the judge I was going in front of, was a damn good food customer of mine for about two years. I sat in his living room many times having scotch and listening to him play his bagpipes. He sucked at it, but I laughed and smiled and drank scotch with him. I had dinner with him and his wife. They were connected with my group of wealthy customers - the clique, in which I had every clique in every town back in those days.

Oh my God, this story is just getting started! OK, we are standing in front of Judge Taylor. My family decided to go get a high-powered attorney named P. Brickens from Baltimore and Frederick, Maryland. The district attorney made his case about "me" Al Capone driving into his small town once a month and dropping off tons of drugs. Oh my God I thought! This is bullshit. My attorney pushes back and told the truth.

You should have seen this seventy-year-old sophisticated judge, my friend. With a solemn look after hearing both sides, he jokes.

He says, "I wonder if I'm under investigation." He starts laughing. He liked me a lot. And he knew I wasn't a drug dealer. This was a very intense time. Footnote: my mother and father let my grandmother live with them. She had a lot of money. My mother was her power of attorney. That is how I got my lawyer. He was amazing, a total professional.

Everyone in my crowd was angry, my two friends, their parents, and my parents. I was sick. I literally was going through major withdrawal. Before the bail hearing for days, I lay in jail. I was throwing up, sweating. It was horrific. I could only classify it as "hell on earth." You'll be hearing that a good bit. Withdrawal from opiates is "hell on earth" for many reasons.

Judge Taylor recused himself due to being a customer of mine and a friend. My lawyer asked for a change of venue due to all the mitigating circumstance, the small town, and everybody knowing me. So it was changed to Cumberland, Maryland.

Well, get ready for this twist. The Honorable Judge Shar of Cumberland County, Maryland and his lovely wife were also great customers of mine! You can't make this up. I had been sent to them by Judge Taylor and his wife. I had been selling food and jewelry to them for years. The judge in Cumberland kept this a secret. My lawyer told me to shut up. You do not look a gift horse in the mouth. Well, my attorney had to plead me guilty. I was caught red handed and they had me dead to rights.

My attorney, Mr. Brickens and I planned everything out. I got out on bail and went to Gateway Rehabilitation (my first rehab finally) in order to show the judge, I wanted to get better. Then they told me to get records from the Indiana Hospital and Dr. Berkeley. The date for a sentencing hearing was set and the district attorney was not budging from twenty years. I asked my attorney if it was ok for Judge Shar to hold this hearing. Judge Shar was a good decent man. He knew I wasn't a drug dealer like the DA made me out to be.

So I went to Gateway Rehab around 1986. Thirty days in and then my parents picked me up. We went out to a damn restaurant and got drunk. Back then, everyone thought I was cured. I felt great. It was time to drink. I had no idea what addiction meant. I had no idea how easy it was to relapse. Basically, I go home and get ready for the hearing. My uncles came down to testify on my behalf. I spent years with them going hunting and fishing and we had a great rapport. I was a good kid.

Attorney Brickens was amazing, tying everything together, that is, with my food business, the breaking of my leg, and Dr. Berkeley, a morphine addict in prison for involuntary manslaughter for killing his wife. I got on the stand and told my story, the truth. A handful of upstanding citizens from Oakland, Maryland came and testified on my behalf. These were great people. And the medical records from the Indiana Hospital revealed everything.

People in the court were amazed at the number of opioids I had received on a daily basis for months and then over a year in a cast afterwards. Judge Shar knew my story and knew I was a good guy. He gave me a two-year sentence with work release to start right away. This was important. Cumberland, Maryland was an hour and twenty minutes from where I lived. I was to be let out every morning at 7:00 am, drive home, run my steak and seafood and jewelry business and come back to jail. I was clean at this time. My life was good. I started with a new kind of vitality. I could run my home delivery steak and seafood/ jewelry business while serving my sentence. I was saved. Well, get ready. Things don't happen this easy. Buckle up.

My sentence was ready to start. My father drives me down to Cumberland. You see, they gave me a month before I had to start my jail sentence. I am in front of the jail and he drops me off. This was very unsettling, but the positive thing is I would be getting out on work release right away. This kept me from having a nervous breakdown. There is no way I can describe the fear, the sheer terror I felt sitting in dad's car, staring at the outside of this prison! You watch movies and hear all these horrific stories about what goes on inside prison walls.

A Lieutenant Gold was sitting at his desk when I entered. He was glaring at me as I walked in! He didn't like me from the beginning. Here he was best friends with the Oakland district attorney and they got together and decided to give me my due justice, his own justice. The district attorney was pissed off I only got two years. I was thrown in a cell and day after day went by with no work release. Weeks go by still no work release. My attorney gets involved.

"This is my jail," says Lieutenant Gold, "I decide when."

Gold and the DA were working together to keep me in as long as they could. Sixty-five days go by. Judge Shar gets pissed, goes to the jail himself, and threatens to fire Lieutenant Gold. I am released immediately for work release.

CHAPTER 4
WORK RELEASE: UNLEASH THE BUSINESSMAN

Well, Lieutenant Gold was pissed but he had to let me out on my work release. Boy was I ready. That little stay for sixty-five days-only allowed out to shower every three days-was disgusting. I mean I felt like an animal. So I'm out every morning by 7 AM and I had to be back at eight in the evening. I thought that was pretty good. I would drive home in the morning, load my truck, and drive to Clearfield, State College, or one of my areas. I would take my jewelry with me and start selling. I would make sure I got back to my house in Newry, PA by about six to make phone calls for the next day. And I got a system down where I had it working really well. In fact, all I was allowed to do was work. They checked my sales receipts and "piss tested" me. I'm just going to say they "piss tested" me for any partying whatsoever. Lieutenant Gold at first was trying to find a way to get me knocked off work release. And I was being a good boy. I was doing the right thing. I actually was building my business up. That's all I could do.

On weekends we weren't allowed out on work release. So every weekend we had to stay in this one room they gave for the work release people. And after a while I actually befriended guards, and even Lieutenant Gold was coming around. They would let me bring in lobster tails, King Crab legs, and steaks. We had our own little stove in work release section. And I'd bring in all this delicious food and also X-rated tapes. There were only guys in there and we would have like a party thru the weekend. It actually got to be ok. We worked hard all week out on work release. So on the weekends there were about nine of us. We'd sit around, eat seafood, steaks and watch X-rated movies. Oh my, I turned that place around.

And then every Friday they had a sale on pizza at Fox's pizza. I usually made pretty good money during the week. So what I would do was order maybe ten to twelve or fourteen large pizzas for the rest of the jail and boy did those guys enjoy that. I got liked by everybody there. I mean when you're locked up all the time and don't have any money, a piece of pizza is the creme de la creme. It's like the best food you can eat. I felt bad for these guys who weren't as lucky as me to get work release. The whole jail was partying. Friday nights were great!

Anyways, weeks passed and here there were these two female prison guards that would take over on weekends. They noticed me and got to know me. All I can say is things happened. As I said, I'd have to take a urinalysis test when I came in Friday evening and they would administer it to me. Here comes a crazy twist. The next thing I know is I'm thrown in a room. They told me to go in this one room and stay there till they came in. They told me they have ways of getting me off work release that no one would know about. They said they could spike my urine with anything like alcohol, pain pills, and Valium. And I asked, "Why would you do this to me?" "Why are you threatening me?" The heavy-set nasty guard spoke up. "We want you to be our sex slave." I could not believe she just said that. Well, I had to do certain things that they enjoyed. I was basically raped! The two female prison guards would do this about every three to four weeks. Even though I was aroused and excited, this was not something I particularly wanted. But from a male's point of view, it wasn't too difficult and I managed to get thru it. They would drink and get very kinky knowing they had a slave that could not say a damn word. The big one was kinky as hell and got a kick out of smothering me! Not too pleasant.

Now if you believe in Karma! I do! About a year later I'm watching a television show "America's Most Wanted." Here it shows the arrest of a female prison guard and a convict from the Cumberland County Jail!

They were arrested up in Canada! It was her! "Katy", the heavy set, dirty, kinky female prison guard who took way too much pleasure from sitting on my face; smothering me! Making me stay down there underneath her disgusting, smelly ass! She fell in love with a prisoner, broke him out, and they both got caught! I pray she is sitting in her cell reading my book! I am smiling as I write this. Karma is a bitch Katy!

So anyways, I spent nine months on work release and built up a beautiful customer base. I actually increased all my areas with tons of new customers. It was a two-year sentence and my attorney called the judge and asked for a sentence reduction. They're allowed to do this. Judge Shar, who was a customer of mine, said he would think about it. Weeks went by and nothing happened. I was doing work release and thought I had about thirteen more months. All of a sudden, I was released. You see, what Judge Shar did to not make it suspicious was to wait about three weeks after my lawyer had talked to him! I got up one morning to get ready to leave the prison for work release and they said, "No, you're out of here for good." I couldn't believe it! I was released! Judge Shar let me go after nine months. This was amazing! I was never so happy. In fact, I went on a single's cruise to the Caribbean afterwards. That was going to be my little treat for going thru nine months of jail and work release. So I go on this cruise. I was clean, healthy, and felt great. I had saved a lot of money. Jail was a blessing. Let the good times roll!

So you don't think I could get in too much trouble on a cruise. Well, here comes the adventurist side of me. Two of my best friends went with me and we were in Cozumel, Mexico. We just got off the ship. I met a few people that night before and they came with me.

I said, "We're not going to go with the regular tourist bus. We're going to have our own adventure."

I rented a Jeep. Everyone got in. Then we took off down this road, into the freakin' jungle! I mean I just took off out of the town not knowing where the hell I was going. We are in Mexico and I could've cared less. I felt invincible.

So we're driving down the damn road. All of a sudden, three people come out of the jungle. They're standing right in the middle of the road. I stop. Four other people come out behind us, Mexican banditos. I mean they had the damn bullets down the chest, they had the rifles, AK-47s and machetes. These guys do not look happy.

"What you doing? What you doing?" says the one guy.

I mean we all thought we were dead. The people we met the night before on the ship wished they would've never met me. So I had to think quick. We had a couple bottles of whiskey. I held them up. "Here, take this." I started talking to the one gentleman who understood English. I had about a grand in my pocket and threw him out $200 American dollars which was worth a lot more back then in Mexico. We started taking shots of whiskey with them and we actually became friends with these Mexican banditos!

I said, "Where's the craziest place we could go around here to have fun and just unwind?" Well, the leader of the pack gave me directions. We drank another shot with them and took off. Now we ended up in this sweet building with three different bands playing. The building was huge and made a semicircle with a courtyard in the middle. A couple hundred people were seated at the tables. There were two stories and three stages for bands. The waiters were all in suits, very classy. The women were lavishly decorated in jewelry. Everyone there seemed wealthy. The three bands played and up above were all these hotel rooms. The place was beautiful and here we are running right into it. I yelled out to my friends, "Let's play the role." I had a suit jacket on that day and we were all dressed nice. We walked in and pretended we owned the place. Here, every hour all the bands would stop and sixty beautiful women would line up. Well, now I know what the hotel rooms up above were. You took your pick of any woman you wanted every hour on the hour. And I mean they were young Mexican senoritas, totally beautiful.

So needless to say, I partook. Fred, a gentleman I met the night before on the cruise, decided to have a contest with me. I took seven different women to seven different rooms. Fred stopped after five. So I won but I didn't win. The last two women I took into a room, I did not touch. Nothing worked anymore. I said, "I am no good," and we just talked. I enjoyed just communicating with them. I told a few jokes. But I had to play my role as the big stud of course. Those were the days, my friends. And after the cruise, my life was right on track.

CHAPTER 5

LIFE ON THE LAMB: GO WEST YOUNG MAN

OK now, fast forward a few years. I was using again. I had no guidance. I figured I was cured. I started partying again and took a few pills thinking I could handle it and you can't. One is too many and a thousand isn't enough and I can attest to that. That is a fact. So I'm off to the races again, but I'm still doing great with my businesses. My jewelry display was growing. I only owed $50,000 on my $200,000 home. I was making money. The businesses were just flourishing. You see, opioid addiction is so much more dangerous and insidious than we think. You can be clean for a year, two years. But if you do not keep your guard up or do not stay very aware, you will relapse. If you take one opioid and are an opioid addict, then you might as well give everything you worked for away.

Once I was used to the opioid's euphoria, everything else was secondary. Alcohol just made me tired. This was in the eighties and pain pills were everywhere. Opioids became my drug of choice. All the other drugs became what is known as "gateway drugs." You see, I had no clue that once you open the door and start dabbling with your drug of choice, it's just a matter of time. Even one Percocet per week will slowly turn into more and more. You will eventually get back to where you were before you became clean. This is called "progression." You can never start again. Progression kills many addicts!

I started a rock and roll band within these couple years. The bass player needed a place to stay so I took him in. I was good to him. My life was going wonderfully. I was dating a girl named Kim and we would see each other three to four times a week. She was helping my mother at the jewelry store that I gave to mom and dad. They became best friends. And I was building up my own jewelry display. I was still delivering jewelry to my customers that I kept separate from the jewelry store. So it was a good time in my life. Besides the opioid maintenance program, I was on, I was still forging ahead. I was still a good businessman. I still had a life.

So this bass guitar player that moved in to my house was with me for a while. We had a pretty damn good band. Pat was his name. We would practice at my house once or twice a week. We started playing the nightclubs. It's not like I needed another business but this to me was exciting. I was the lead singer. I bought a lot of top-notch sound equipment. And other high-quality musicians joined. It was a good thing. I actually thought I could make something of myself as a singer too. Why not? I was pretty good.

So anyways I'm selling food, selling jewelry, having jewelry shows, dating Kim, starting a rock and roll group...not much going on! And I didn't smoke pot and I never sold pot or marijuana. I had no use for marijuana. But Pat was always bringing up this field of marijuana that he knew of in West Virginia, a gigantic field that was growing wild, that no one else knew about except a few people, Pat being one of them.

I said, "Well OK, "I don't need marijuana, Pat."

"No," he said, "I'll give you Hefty trash bags full for $500 a trash bag."

And I'm thinking why do I want a freakin' trash bag full of marijuana. I don't smoke it. I don't want to sell it. I'm making enough money.

Well, there's more to this story and there's another twist coming. So buckle up everyone. Now the Percocet are getting to me. I'm starting to need more. My opioid addiction was getting worse by the week. I couldn't work quite as much. My energy level was going down but I still had a ton of it.

One day, this friend I used to get Percocet from, says, "Hey, have you heard anything about this field of marijuana?"

I said, "Yeah, I know how to get it. I have a connection."

He said, "Oh my God, I've been trying to find somebody. I'll take ten Hefty trash bags full and I'll give you $1,500 a trash bag."

I said, "What?"

He said, "Yeah, I'll give you $1,500 for every bag. I can get $3,000 per bag. I'll take them. Can you get them?"

Well here comes my businessman mentality... I pay $500, Vinnie will give me $1,500, so ten trash bags full of marijuana -I'll make $10,000.

So I said "OK, I'll get it for you -only if you give me 100 Percocet."

That he agreed to. That's what I really wanted, plus the cash was nice. Like I said, I was getting sicker with my disease and I wasn't working quite as well. So $10,000 I would take. Well, I was young and stupid plus addicted to drugs. So why the hell wouldn't I do that. OK here we go, I was easy prey for law enforcement. They want to look good and they want their busts to be big. You think I would've learned my lesson after the Oakland, Maryland incident. But when you're addicted to opioids, you don't really think of any setbacks. You don't care. You live for the day.

Now Pat who was working with me as a bass player in my band was also working for the drug task force. In other words, Pat was a "snitch" trying to make busts to get out of his problems. And Vinnie, who wanted the marijuana, this is ridiculous, was also a fucking "snitch." So, the guy bringing the marijuana and the guy taking the marijuana were both "snitches" working for the police. The reason the police wanted me was because of Pat's bullshit making me look like this big drug kingpin- all lies. He saw I had expensive things in my home. He saw I was doing well. And what sucks about that is I was working my butt off. I always had a great work ethic. I had the home delivery food going. I had the home delivery jewelry going right along with it. I had jewelry parties, jewelry shows. In one day, I could sell a $10,000 diamond and make three grand. And I was doing that. Most of my food customers were very well to do. They could afford lobster tails, shrimp. And the jewelry went hand in hand. When I had the jewelry parties, these ladies went crazy! I just brought the wine, got them a little tipsy and it was "buy, buy, buy. "

Anyways, we finally get a break and are supposed to go to Baltimore with our band and sign a contract to play in a big nightclub down there. This was going to happen in about a week. First, I wanted to get this pot deal through. To me it was a done deal. Both people had connections and money.

So I set it up.

I said, "Pat, bring me ten bags on a Friday night and I'll give you $5,000 cash, $500 a bag." Then I contacted Vinnie and said, "Vinnie, you come over Saturday morning about 10 o'clock. I want $1,500 a bag. There's going to be ten trash bags full of marijuana."

Easy money I thought- done deal. Pat brings the bags. I pay him Friday night. Vinnie also dropped off 100 free Percocet two days before that. (The police say they never knew about the Percocet! Do I believe them? NOPE!)

So anyways, the next morning 10 AM, I'm hungover sitting at my table in the living room. No shirt on, I'll never forget this, hair was a mess, just waiting on Vinnie. I was very relaxed waking up. A knock comes to my door. I opened it and there's Vinnie. I look behind him and I kid you not. A whole SWAT team of police with rifles, pistols wearing vests, were running right behind Vinnie. There were fifteen to twenty of them streaking to my door.

Vinnie's greatest line, I'll never forget this, was "What did you do, call the cops on me?" Son of a bitch. I was good to him and Pat too.

Here we go. At age thirty-two, I was back in the clutches of the law. And this, my friends, is one of the biggest side effects of opioid addiction. You will always have brushes with the law. You will always get in trouble. You have no conscience. You are not yourself.

Well, the cops take me in their office. The whole thing was a damn setup. Sonny was the head honcho, the chief of the drug task force. When they raided my house, they didn't find much. I had a safe with $2,000 in it, some musical instruments, just a typical house except a warehouse on the side of it with freezers full of food. They did find the Percocet that Vinnie brought over before. It was illegal. But when you're working for the cops, they don't give a shit about what you do as a "snitch". They turn their heads. You can do anything you want as long as you get them a bust. That's why they love "snitches" so they don't have to do the hard dangerous work. It's nuts.

I'm in the office and they weighed the pot. It was twenty-two pounds.

Sonny's looking at me saying "You're in a big heap of trouble, boy. We could charge you for this now and you would definitely get some pretty long jail time."

I'm thinking to myself. *Everything was too easy. I just figured out that both Vinnie and Pat were "snitches"- sitting right there talking to Sonny. Isn't that entrapment?* Well, I found out later, as long as you are a willing participant, they can get by it.

Then Sonny looks at me in the office and says, "Here's what we're going to do. You're going to go home for a month. We're not going to charge you. We're just going to let you go home. In about thirty days, we want you to take down everyone you know selling or participating in drugs."

I did know a lot of people- in eight different towns. When you are in the opioid world, you meet everybody sooner or later-cocaine dealers, heroin dealers. You name it. You come across it. A lot of them are addicted to opioids also. So I'm thinking to myself, *If I become a "snitch", I'm dead! I better take my time and think this over.*

I said, "Sonny, OK, you got a deal. Just let me go and get my shit together. And in thirty days, I'm going to make some busts for you."

Then I went home and said to myself, "Nope, nope, nope, ain't going to do that."

Talk about a twist coming up here. Time to start a new life! Time to leave.

I don't want to spend years in jail which I thought was going to happen to me at the time. So I decided to "take off out west young man!"

I found a seventeen-year-old hippie. "Beaner" was his nickname. He lived in California but was out here visiting friends and he wanted to go back. So we made plans.

I said, "Beaner, how about me coming with you. We'll take our time getting to California and we'll go our separate ways..."

You see, I planned it out with my girlfriend that I would take off with "Beaner" and change my name to "Jeffrey Scott". Start over again. She would come out and meet me six months later and we would start a new life. What a time!

Now I gave everything to my parents. I took about $40,000 in jewelry, $5,000 in cash, my clothes and my stereo system, had to take my stereo system. It took up the whole damn trunk. So Beaner and I leave. We're on the road. It was sad and surreal, but very exciting, kind of like...time to start a new life- an adventure!

Now, ladies and gentlemen, here's the only thing I hadn't thought about. I loaded up on Percocet and anything else I could find, Vicodin, etc. I thought I would be OK and I could manage my opioid addiction. But I was taking that monkey on my back. I was taking the biggest problem on the planet. So you will see later how you can succeed when you're addicted. It's terrible. Now we take off. And I'll never forget, once we leave Pennsylvania, this big weight lifted off my chest. I could feel it. All of a sudden, I felt lighter, happier, free and did we have a time heading to California.

We stopped in about four different states. The first one was Memphis, TN. We decided to go out. Now I was used to the topless bars and the strip joints around here. And they are ok but nothing too crazy happens while the girls are on the stage. But I was never to a Memphis, TN striptease bar. I'm sitting there giving this southern belle tips. She was in a white mini dress and had black leather boots up to her knees with beautiful long flowing black hair and blue eyes. She was gorgeous.

She said, "Would you like a lap dance?"

I said, "Sure."

Next thing I'm in this booth that you can't see. And she's dancing all around me. Next thing my pants come down and she's on her knees. Unbelievable. I was shocked. Well, every time I would get to a point of a certain excitement, she would hold her hand out. And I would throw her another $20. Needless to say, she held her hand out a few times. I've never had anything like that happen to me in a dance club. And I'll never forget it!

So we take off from Memphis, TN and we decide to make a stop overnight in Amarillo, TX. That, my friends, almost cost me my life. We arrive in Amarillo, find a nightclub, and order some drinks. I look around. All the guys wore Stetson hats, white shirts, blue jeans and boots. Every guy looked the same. The women were dressed in minidresses and nice jeans and they all looked hot. This blonde comes up to me and starts hitting on me. I start buying her drinks. Beaner is sitting there smiling. Next thing we're dancing and slow dancing.

And as we're sitting at our table, one of the clones, one of the guys, came over to me and whispered.

"So, this is Amarillo Truck Stop, huh. We know you're out of town and we don't like out of towners coming here thinking they can have our women."

Well, me, I looked up at him and I said, "Thank you for your opinion. Glad you told me that. Now leave me alone or you'll get hurt."

Bad, bad, bad thing to say. The girl's sitting on my lap. Hours went by. Next thing I know everyone's surrounding me. About twenty guys make a circle around my table and are staring right at me. Beaner is scared shitless. The girl gets up. I actually told her to get up and leave for now. The next thing, I saw guys getting pissed and talking to each other. A few of them leave. The band breaks up. The owner comes over in twenty minutes.

He says "Listen, I know what they're up to. Here in Texas, they'll take you out and disappear you."

I looked out the window and noticed pickup trucks driving around the damn building. It was close to closing with guys in the back just whooping and hollering.

The owner insisted, "You guys better get some protection because these boys mean business. They are pissed and they're going to do something."

So I called the cops. Thank God I called the cops! They were even afraid. They came over and they backed us up until we got to our motel room. And I'm telling you when we walked outside, those boys were ready for business. They were not faking it. I saw ropes.

People were chugging beer, screaming, "Get the outsiders. Stay out of Amarillo!"

Somehow, we made it back to our room. But I looked out the window every twenty minutes. Thank God the police car was sitting parked outside our building. That's how scared they were of the situation. They were on high alert. So we made it out of that one.

Time to get up early in the morning and leave Amarillo. I want to relay a footnote. When I say I'm addicted again, it seems like I'm always clean for a little bit. Then I say I'm addicted again. Well, what happens is not that simple. You might have a tooth pulled. And if you're clean for a long time, back then you thought you were ok. You thought you could handle a few pain pills. And I'm pretty sure that's what got me addicted the last time. I got twelve Percocet for having a molar pulled. And that started the ball rolling. Once you open that door, it might take weeks or months but you will become addicted again.

You have a disease! It is a fact.

Total abstinence is the only way you can go. I tried NA. I tried AA. In fact, I went there many times. But with my life, my businesses and working as hard as I did, I didn't really have time to go there enough. That might have saved me back then but I had to build a life. I was very energetic and busy. A lot of people in the meetings didn't work and were on welfare. A lot of people had to quit their jobs; they hit bottom. So it's not really a motivating place. Anyways for me it wasn't.

You see, that field of marijuana back in West Virginia. -the cops had been using that field for years. They were male plants, had no THC in them. But it was pot and that was their way to bust people. If I would've fought it, I might've won. But instead, I decided to do this. I decided to take off and start over again. I was tired of courts and judges and all that bullshit. So I make it to California. Beaner goes to his family, lets me off in San Francisco. Kim is secretly on her way, leaving Pennsylvania.

My father confronted the cops and told them I took off, "My son is gone." He said he had no idea where I had gone to and what I was doing.

Sonny was irate, "He'll be back. He'll get caught out there. It's just a matter of time."

Kim finally makes it to California. It was so nice seeing her. It was probably after three months of leaving home. We had a lot of feelings for each other. So we met in Oakland right across the bay from San Francisco. It was about seven in the evening. I'll never forget that evening, 78 degrees and sunny.

We were on the Oakland Beach. You could look over at San Francisco and see the skyscrapers. And the sun was going down hitting them with this beautiful side angle shot. They had this gorgeous reddish bluish tint to them with the angle of the sun. It was absolutely surreal.

I had bought this big map of the United States. I laid it down on the sand.

I said, "Kim, you came with me, had faith in me. Point anywhere on this map you want to go to make a new life."

Tucson, Arizona, bam. No questions asked. And little did this opioid addict know that Tucson was the cocaine capital of the world at the time; Nogales, Mexico was forty minutes away. The borders are very porous. That will come up later. We had an epic evening, took off the next day.

Tucson, Arizona here we are. We decided to check out their flea markets. Tucson has flea markets all year round. And they're high-class flea markets. People sell good stuff. I had a $40,000 jewelry display that I could make look like $300,000. We set it out. And right away we did amazingly well. We weren't getting rich but we were selling $400, $600, $1,000 a day which is a nice profit with jewelry. You see the Mexicans in Tucson don't buy Mexican jewelry. It's 10kt. but in reality, it's about 3 or 4 or 5kt. Bootlegging is everywhere. So Mexicans with a lot of money come up and buy their jewelry in America- the good stuff, quality control, 14kt, 18kt. So we tore up.

We got this beautiful villa condominium. There were about thirty of them in a circle- with a swimming pool, a tennis court, a weight room, and a laundromat for everyone to use- $475 a month. It was just perfect for us. Back then, they were opening up the first indoor swap meet in the country, in other words, a gigantic mall. But inside it's a big high class flea market where you have straw and booths. People were selling leather and gold and anything you can imagine. There were hundreds of booths there so we signed up and got one. We met some friends. Tucson, Arizona was becoming a nice home for us. At first, mom and dad would send me out some jewelry to increase our stock. Then I found a distributor in Tucson and basically, I was on my own.

We had our own life started. Oh, oh no, we didn't. No, we didn't. That monkey on my back was turning into a gorilla. I only had a few pills left. I was only taking the very, very minimum and I was not feeling well. I was starting to get sick. This damn disease is terrible. Every day you must have a certain amount.

So we're at the swap meet. It opens up. We had these great neighbors who sold leather purses, leather belts, nice quality stuff -right beside us. They were Mexicans from Nogales. And there was Antonio, the twenty-year-old son who befriended us. He would come over every day and buy $1,000 worth, $2,000 worth. And his dad would come over. His mom would come over. Big money. They were making us well to do.

One day he says, "Do you like cocaine?"

I said, "Sure, why not."

Maybe it would help with my opioid withdrawal. It doesn't. He brings in a chunk of cocaine the next day and it was worth $400 to $500. And he just gives it to me. I couldn't believe it. These people are wealthy.

CHAPTER 6

Arrested in Tucson:
TIME TO DO THE IMPOSSIBLE

I'm working the jewelry store one day. I'm sick. So I decided to go doctor shopping. I told Kim I was going to Old Tucson to look at the old city and maybe get into some stuntman work. I was in great shape and I actually had done some stunts earlier and they told me to come back. But I went doctor shopping. I'm sweating. I'm a day in to my withdrawal so I'm half out of my mind. I sit there in his office and the doctor takes me to an examining room and leaves. He's gone for twenty minutes. I look down and there's a script book. I reached over and took two scripts out and put them in my pocket. I was half insane at the time, didn't give a shit. He comes back and I talk him into writing me out a script for Vicodin. My back was never good. That injury I had eight years ago screwed my nerves up at the base of my spine or whatever. It did hurt somewhat. You become very good at finding injuries and making them up.

So the twelve Vicodin didn't last too long. And I decided to forge a script. I got his name perfect. I got the signature perfect. I went into a pharmacy and got thirty Percocet, no problem at all. I left, went on my merry way. Life was good for a while. I went to another doctor and got a legitimate script. For some reason in Tucson, they hadn't figured it out yet. Opioids weren't big out there. I think it was more heroin and cocaine so we could really bullshit doctors easy. It hadn't reached that part of the country yet. If you told them you were in ten-scale pain, you got some damn good shit. They had a black tar problem.

About six weeks had passed and I go to the same pharmacy that I took that forged script to. Now mind you, the jewelry store is doing great. We love our condominium. We have friends. We're having dinner with people. Well, I walk in and ten minutes, twenty minutes, thirty minutes went by - waiting on them to fill this legitimate script. Next thing I know, my arms were flailed back and handcuffs were thrown on me. I'm taken in a paddy wagon and I'm in Pima County Jail, Tucson, Arizona. Here, Percocet are a schedule one narcotic, ladies and gentlemen. And the doctors must follow up after each visit with a phone call from the pharmacy. They will call the doctor and verify the script.

Well, the doctor said, "No, I did not write that script."

They had my picture in the pharmacy. If I would've never went back there, I would probably have never got in trouble. It's so busy in the city and it was close to the condo I was living in.

So I'm in the Pima County Jail. Jeffrey Scott's my name. I didn't come up on their computers on the national data base. There was no Jeffrey Scott especially with the social security number I gave them. But I fit the profile of a criminal that they were after, some murderer who they hadn't caught yet, who looked like me and they thought I was him.

Bam! Boom! All of a sudden, a baton to the gut, a baton to the back.

"Who are you? What's your name?" Throwing me against the lockers. And I kid you not. I'm in this damn room and they are kicking my butt. This was "their" jail. This was their county. They pretty well ran the place and they wanted an answer. Well, I broke! I wasn't going to get my ass kicked and maybe be wounded for life. They were doing a number on me.

"Craig Weaver's my name."

Well, here Sonny had waited a good while before he put my charges up in the national data base. Two days before I went into the pharmacy and got busted, he puts it in. They knew everything about me.

1-I was wanted for marijuana in PA. # 2-Fleeing from justice. # 3 - I was on probation five years in Oakland, Maryland for the cocaine incident that the judge was nice enough to let me out in nine months instead of two years. #4 a damn forgery of a prescription in Tucson, a third-degree felony.

I contacted my attorney on the phone. He told me a seventeen-year minimum is what I'm looking at with all the charges I had. I called Kim the next day and told her where I was. I had to go for a bail hearing. I got turned down- no bail-since I was out of state and had charges on me. Kim was frantic.

Ultimately, I sat down and realized I'd hit a low point of my life, I mean LOW. What do I do now? Where do I go? Where do I turn? But I believed my cup is still half full no matter what situation I get into. I spent days thinking in my cell. I knew Antonio, the Mexican family's son, was involved in one of the biggest drug cartels in Nogales, Mexico. He was the delivery guy to Chicago and Los Angeles. His dad and his uncle ran the cartel with tons of other relatives, bodyguards. They were delivering 300 kilos a week to Chicago, 300 kilos a week to Los Angeles. And the store in the mall was just a front.

Now Antonio would look up to me and tell me stories. One day he was driving through Mexico and entering into the United States and the "federales" pulled him over. He said they found the cocaine, a truckload.

I said, "What happened?'

"I had to give them my truck." he says.

And his truck was worth $50,000. It was a top notch GNC beautiful truck.

I said, "That was the payoff?"

"Yes."

"What did you do then?"

"I got a new truck," says Antonio and he started laughing.

I mean money was nothing. OK, this cartel was huge. And I'm sitting in the Pima County Jail looking at a seventeen-year minimum mandatory sentence.

It hit me and I had an epiphany! Back in those days, in my mind there wasn't anything I could not do if I put my mind to it. My adrenalin was running wild. Even though I was going through withdrawal, I was so pumped, I overrode it. My youth played a big role.

Dammit, I'm going to bust that drug cartel. I have to. They're hurting people, even though I liked Antonio. I didn't know the uncle too well. But they're hurting a lot of people. I can take them down.

You see, I had told Antonio on one of the days that we were bullshitting that I had a friend who was a big distributor in PA. I did know someone, the person who gave me the ounce for Oakland, Maryland. He got his cocaine from Florida and he wasn't happy with it. I had been talking to Antonio before about that.

And he said, "Get him out here. We will hook him up. Fly him out and have him rent a car and drive back. No problem."

So we had already discussed that. Back then I was just making conversation. But now it will come to fruition.

So I'm sitting in the Pima County Jail. I'm figuring everything out. I can do this. At the same time, Mexicans hate Americans in Pima County. When you're in jail, they have gangs in there. I was called a "gringo." Well, two Mexican gangs were after me to be their "bitch." I was supposed to carry a guy's tray up the day before and of course I refused. And I was getting bad looks from everyone. I mean they had to teach me a lesson sooner or later and I knew it was coming. So I had my bust all figured out. I was on GO!

Now I just had to get the guard's attention and talk them in to letting me see a cop, someone in charge, to get out of there. This was my biggest challenge.

I would call a guard over and say, "Listen, I can bust a drug cartel. I can take it down. I need out."

They steered away from me for a while. I actually scared them to death. They thought I was crazy.

"Keep your mouth shut in here!" they said, "If anyone else hears you, you are dead."

I kept trying to convince them. I talked to three different guards in a matter of two weeks.

"Let me talk to somebody. I can do this," I said, "I have an 'in' with a drug cartel from Nogales, Mexico. They're shipping tons of cocaine up into the states."

The guards would look at me and just tell me to shut the fuck up.

So two weeks go by, a guard comes up, "Mr. Weaver, come with me."

"Where are we going?" I asked.

"Just shut up and come with me. Your attorney's here," he says.

I don't have an attorney, I thought.

"Just shut up Mr. Weaver."

He takes me down into this room. I mean this jail was huge. Two stories down, I go into to this dark room, no lights. It looked like an interrogation room.

Here sits this shady looking character, long hair, beard, "biker dude" type, dark sunglasses in a dark room.

"I'm an undercover agent. What do you have for me? Don't waste my time," he says.

I was thinking quickly. I have to convince this guy right now. This is the most important meeting of my life.

Craig, do not screw this up! I thought.

Well, I laid everything out to him. I told him I was on the run from a pot deal, step by step how I got in the swap meet mall, how I met Antonio, his family and just how big they were.

I said, "Listen, this guy's bringing me in lots of pure coke at the mall worth $500, $800 and just giving it to me. And I was giving him good prices on gold, of course. "

And the undercover cop said, "How do you know he's going to listen to you? How do you know you can get him to sell you something?"

I said, "Well, in a few conversations that I had with Antonio, I did mention this guy in Altoona, Pennsylvania that was a big cocaine dealer, the biggest in our area. And I told Antonio that he would go to Florida, pick up his cocaine and that I could probably get him to come out here."

The undercover cop's just sitting there staring at me. I had no idea what this guy was thinking. I played it over and over in my head.

I said to the man, "I know I can talk Antonio into bringing me a shipment."

Well, very few words from this guy. Our conversation was over. They led me back up to my cell.

And I thought, "OK, that was good but what the hell?"

Well in the next two days I was out. The judge instructed the court to take jewelry as collateral. Kim went over and took care of that. Two days later I am back at the villa trying to settle Kim down. Now mind you I'm going through withdrawal. I'm sick but my adrenalin was pumping like a son of a bitch. I manage to find some pain pills. This was not going to be easy. I had to let Kim know what was going on. She knew something was wrong with me and actually suspected that I was taking pills. It wears you down. Trying to hide your addiction is not easy. Everyone sooner or later suspects you and Kim knew I was sick. Your personality can change on a dime.

So I was contacted by the undercover cop. I told him to give me a few days to get back with Antonio and his family. He said OK and gave me his number. The next day I was back at the swap meet.

Antonio comes running over, "Where have you been? What was wrong? You sick?" in broken English.

"I had pneumonia," I told him, "A bad case of it but I'm better now. Everything's back to normal, Antonio."

He was glad. Antonio was not a bad kid- twenty years old, good looking, very intelligent. Well, I didn't hit him up that day about my drug buddy wanting to come out and buy some kilos of cocaine.

But the next morning I went into the store and I said, "Antonio, you remember I told you about my cocaine dealer in Altoona?"

He said, "Yes, I do."

I said, "Well, he's very unhappy with his last shipment. It was only 80% pure."

Antonio went off, "Get him out here! Get him out here! We will give you 99% pure. Our stuff is the best. I will take you to meet my family tomorrow."

Well, the next day, Antonio picks me up in a limousine and takes me to Nogales, Mexico. I was nervous. But I had to play my role. Women everywhere. I'm out on the veranda overlooking Nogales, Mexico in this beautiful mansion. I was staying calm, cool, and collected. I sit down. There's his father, his uncle, and girls running around bringing me cocktails, Mexican senoritas with almost nothing on. Little kids were running around and there were bodyguards. I couldn't believe it. I am in a movie, I chuckled. I was made for this. Well, I did calm down. The role was not hard to play especially with these hot looking Mexican senoritas shoving their breasts in my face serving me a cocktail. No, this wasn't that hard.

So I told everybody at the table about my drug dealing buddy. I told them he wanted ten kilos. The dad and the uncle questioned me and everything went well.

They said, "OK, we will give you a try. You bring him out here next weekend- next Saturday. You tell him to fly out and we will get him a vehicle to drive back."

"Okay," I said.

Then I went home the next morning after a very interesting evening. Let's just say I had a hard night, a very long night.

Kim was very "pissed" at me. She thought something went on, but of course, I calmed her down. I said I got too drunk to come back and nobody could drive. This house they lived in was worth millions. It sat on top of a mountain looking down at the poverty-stricken city of Nogales. These people had money, lots of it. $50,000 trucks parked everywhere, Corvettes, nice cars.

Antonio was a jokester. At night, he brought out a pet monkey they had. It was pretty cool. It kept slapping me on the head.

Antonio said, "He likes you. If he punches you in the head, he likes you."

I said, "Great!"

I said to Kim, "Get ready, the less you know, the better."

Well, everything went normal at the swap meet. I contacted the Pima County drug task force and got together with them. I told them about the layout of the mansion in Nogales, how many vehicles, how many people around. I gave them as many details as I could. And we came to agreement for ten kilos. I remember kilos back in Altoona going for $30,000 per kilo. Antonio's dad quoted me $20,000. So right off the bat I was getting one hell of a deal, I guess.

I started thinking, *How the hell did I get here?*

Just think if I did not have this little charge on me of forging a script and this was all legitimate. My mind started fantasizing. Even working for the cops without a charge, I would've made a lot of money. And illegally they wanted me to run cocaine for them to Chicago and Los Angeles. They would pay me $10,000 a trip -three days. It sounded great but you always get caught. Always. It does not end well. I still had my demon with me. My addiction was alive and well. The opioids had me. I couldn't function without them.

As the years went by, I became acutely addicted. The withdrawals were worse and the feelings of despair became constant. I had so many bad mornings. When you wake up after sleeping all night, after not taking any pills, your endorphins are not working at all. Especially after sleeping all night, you open your eyes and you can't think. It hurts. You can't move. I used to put my pills on the coffee table beside my bed. And I would set my alarm for an hour before I got up. It would go off. I'd throw them in my mouth, go back to sleep and wake up feeling OK. How bad is that? Actually, how sad is that? This is how I lived. I was a slave to addiction. It was killing me. There were times I wish I could just end it all. There were times I wished I could just get well and get over that mountain. But the withdrawals were terrible. You will be hearing much more about this later. It takes months to free your mind.

So Saturday morning came. Everything was ready. I had just met my undercover cop who was going to be with me for our transaction. A light haired thirty-year-old man wearing a Pittsburgh Steeler hat looked perfect for the Altoona/ Pittsburgh area. I liked him right away. He had a rough edge about him which was good. We got to know each other a little bit that morning. We went over all the information about the case. We were to meet Antonio in the mall parking lot at 11 AM. Everything was set.

Here the day before, Antonio comes up to me in the swap meet and says, "By the way, my dad took the price down to $18,000 per kilo for you."

"Thank you, Antonio. Tell your dad, thank you."

My God, the money to be made on 2.2 pounds 97% pure. Do the math.

I was nervous but I was excited. This was huge. I was involved in something so much bigger than myself, something actually very important. I sort of felt good about everything and felt it was my duty to do this. We all get that sense of well-being when we think we're fighting a just cause, when we're doing something for the good of the community, for the good of the nation. And I was. This was a huge drug cartel. They were poisoning the United States with tons of cocaine every year, tons! And it would be a good thing to get rid of it.

So it's 10 AM Saturday morning, another sunny day in Tucson. I hadn't slept at all and had been on edge driving to the station. But all that tension left once I got there. Here comes the young blond haired undercover cop with his Pittsburgh Steeler ball cap and a briefcase of literally $180,000 cash. I dove into my role and was totally into it. I can remember calmness overwhelming me as I became the main actor in a movie, the helpful person bringing his drug dealer buddy to do good business.

They played it down to the wire. Everything was correct. We walked out to the car. I saw two vans behind the car and a couple other unmarked vehicles.

"SWAT teams," I asked.

"Yes, we need SWAT teams for this."

Everyone was kind of nervous but excited. Adrenalin was in the air. The briefcase was put in the trunk. I was sitting in the passenger seat of the car. The undercover cop drove. When Antonio brought the kilos over, he was to give them to me. And the undercover cop was to get out, tell him the money is in the trunk, and hand him the briefcase. And when that was done, he was to tilt his hat with his left hand. That was the sign - everyone was supposed to converge.

Alright, everything's ready. We pulled in the parking lot. There's Antonio in his car. He was all by himself. I looked around and saw his two uncles and dad in another car and two other vehicles with four men in each vehicle around twenty to thirty yards away. The undercover cop drove. We were sitting there. Antonio comes over with one package. I thought to myself, this is not ten kilos.

He comes over, opens the door, slides in the back seat. It's now 11 AM.

He says, "Here's one kilo. You take it home. You check it out and we will meet back here at 1 o'clock with the other nine."

Now the funny thing that caught me right away was he never asked for any money for the one kilo. He actually trusted me enough to leave with that kilo, an $18,000 item, without anything down. I must've been getting the royal treatment. They really wanted my business. They trusted me. I think it was after six months of seeing, buying all the jewelry, they got very comfortable.

I am very good at getting people to trust me, getting people to become my friend. I've practiced this all throughout my life selling food, selling jewelry. That's what I was good at. Later in life as you're going to read, I will transcend into another world and this is where my gift became my worst nightmare. You see not only was I able to get along amazingly with the elites of the community who would buy all kinds of things off me, I was also excellent at getting along with the animals of society, the oppressed, the very dysfunctional. I had a knack for getting along with them. And basically, what it is I think mainly is to be yourself at all times. Don't filter things. Don't lie. Just say what you think no matter who you're talking to, then everyone knows where you stand. So what took me to success, the gift I have that I honed throughout the years, also took me to a very, very bad place on this planet.

So getting back...we leave with the kilo and go to the police barracks. We took a few wrong turns. We took our time, zig zagging our way back. The undercover cop wanted to make sure Antonio or somebody in his crew didn't follow us. The undercover cop and I walked into headquarters. He throws the kilo up to show everyone. Clapping and cheers erupt.

The secretaries were clapping, "Good job! Good job!"

No one's looking at me. They're looking at him and I'm thinking, *This guy didn't do a damn thing. It was me. Clap for me everyone. Oh well, I am just glad it was going smooth.*

But at this point in time, I forgot to take care of me. What I should've done is had a lawyer ready so when we got that first kilo in headquarters, I could've had anything I wanted. Dammit. I could've had them call Blair County and tell them they would have to drop the charges and clear my slate. But I didn't think of that. I didn't think of me at the time. I was just so damn excited and proud that this thing was going perfect so far. I screwed up big time. I'm too trusting. What I didn't realize is the police are out for themselves. I meant nothing to them. They want as much attention, as many busts as they can get for them to move up. Everyone wants to outdo the other and there's a lot of jealousy that erupts. It's a very tense organization, I found out. I just figured and thought that making this gigantic bust for them was going to clear me of everything. Well, I thought wrong.

See, the only thing that separated these people from me was my disease. Actually, my situation.! To those people, I was a bad person on the wrong side of the law, trying to right my wrongs by doing "good deeds." They thought of me as a criminal and I could feel their negativity. Now in my mind I screwed up to be in this situation, but I was just like them. They were no better than me and I was actually proving that. To be honest, I think I could have been one hell of an undercover cop. I knew my abilities and feel sure they were noticing how I managed to coordinate the situation with the members of the cartel and prison guards. And to be honest, I was running the whole show with the narcotics squad. Talk about logistical multitasking lol. But as you will find out soon, that damn charge I had on me kept me down as a low-life snitch. You know what, they saw it and knew. I saw the stares and looks I was secretly getting. It's a game, a dangerous game at that!

So, we have a kilo and they tested it in their department. It was 98% pure. That is pure cocaine. That's about as pure as you can get. We sit and we sit and we wait.

It's twenty till 1 and we go back. There's Antonio, Antonio's dad and uncles thirty yards away. The body guards were in other cars shooting glares at me. I didn't let it phase me. I was in the mode. I was on script. I was the main character so I had to be tough but calm. That was my mindset. I now sit here in amazement at just what exactly was going down at that time. Antonio comes over. I give him a thumbs up and a smile. He's carrying this four-foot-long Marine duffel bag.

He opens my door, sets it on my lap and says, "Check them."

With a smile, I said, "I don't have to, Antonio. You trusted me with one kilo. I could trust you with quality and everything else."

So now the undercover cop gets out, stands up, "The money's in the trunk."

He heads back, opens the trunk and gets the briefcase out. Antonio's with him and he opens it up, -$180,000 in cash- and he hands it to Antonio. His left hand lifts his hat and tilts it down. That was it. All hell breaks loose. The bust is on. Vans, cars, everybody pulled up and surrounded the perimeter. The bodyguards tried to run. One got shot in the leg so the other one stopped. Two SWAT teams assembled around all the vehicles. Everyone was on high alert, guns everywhere pulled and aimed. It took about two minutes but it seemed like an eternity before they were all detained and everything came together.

Then they had search warrants for not only the one mansion in Nogales but also for one of the uncle's mansions. They found tons of cocaine in each mansion and so much money. The one trooper that was involved in everything was telling me a good bit about it but he couldn't give me specifics. All he told me was that it was the fourth largest bust in the southwestern United States at that time. I felt good. I felt proud.

To be honest with you, the good in me came out and I know I saved a lot of people, actually thousands, not just deaths, but becoming addicted, losing their families. This made me feel like everything was worth it. You see, back then when I was there, Nogales, Mexico was the major cocaine distribution center for the United States.

I was going down to Nogales once a week to see a doctor that got kicked out of the United States. He lost his license for selling pills illegally. He got busted so he decided to traipse down to Mexico and start a business there. I happened to find him while searching for pain pills alias doctor shopping. What the hell, I thought. Nogales was only thirty-eight minutes away from Tucson. So I went down there and the doctor would look at me and say just give me $100. We would go in a room and come back out with Darvocet. Now Darvocet aren't a strong opioid but they are helpful. Let's just say they will keep you from going through withdrawal. And when you're an addict, you'll take anything with opioids in it.

So, I'm sitting in the car while this bust goes on. I see everybody running around all over the place. Finally, the undercover cop and the lieutenant come over to the car and retrieve the duffel bag. They check it right there. Yes, there were nine more kilos of amazing cocaine in there. I'm talking pure cocaine, 97%. You may as well say it's pure. They tell me to go back to my apartment and sit tight, wait for further instructions. That was scary. Antonio knew where I lived. This was no small event. I am sure the cartel wanted me dead by now.

At the mall parking lot, I'll never forget this, when they put Antonio in the police vehicle, we made eye contact. I will be honest. My hair stood up. I felt bad for him, so young, such a nice guy, so intelligent.

He kept looking at me shrugging his shoulders as if to say, "Why? Why did you do this? Why did you destroy our lives?" I could see his lips moving.

Actually, I felt bad but I felt good. He was twenty years old and right up front I asked the lieutenant, "What's he going to get?"

I wasn't too worried about the uncles. They were in their fifties. The hell with them. They knew what they were doing.

The lieutenant looked at me and said, "Due to this being the first time Antonio was busted, but as big as this bust is, he'll probably do seven years, maybe get out in four." That made me feel better. Maybe this is just what Antonio needed.

And now that I'm later up there in years, I do feel good about what I did. I know where Antonio was headed. And it would've only gotten worse. And maybe, just maybe, this gave him a chance at life, real life, a good life. That's what I hope. I would love to see him again. I'd be afraid to, but I would love to see how he's doing, how his life was shaped after his sentence. This is OK. I can live with that. Antonio will be fine.

On a side note, I must come clean. I was sitting there with a 30 lb. cocaine filled duffel bag worth a couple million-dollar street value and I was still sick and in withdrawal. So everyone's running around all pumped with adrenaline and I knew they would be way too wound up and busy to debrief me or even check me. When I was sitting there, I opened up a kilo and shoved pieces of cocaine in my pockets.

Wow. I was doing a good thing for society but I was young, adventurous and definitely no angel back in those days. Let's just say when Kim went to bed, I stayed up and watched tv. Need I say more. I'm sure my eyes were the size of fifty cent pieces the next morning. Now I chuckle, *OMG*.

So Kim and I sat apprehensively in the apartment for one and a half days before the police came. They got me, took me back to the barracks and sat me in front of the big kahuna, the CEO, Sargent or boss whatever you want to call him. He shook my hand and thanked me. He told me they got tons of cocaine out of that bust. The money amount was astronomical. They got to keep the two mansions, tons of vehicles, tons of weapons, and over 250 kilos of cocaine. Now do the math. I got it down to $18,000 per kilo., and it was over 250 kilos and that's wholesale, street value, we're talking millions and millions and millions of dollars. And what sucks, they buried it. I got no credit for it at all except thru police channels which you're going to see and find out didn't serve me very well in Blair County. Honestly, the police could've cared less about me. They wanted to be the heroes. They wanted the glory. And they got it. Just going to headquarters with the undercover cop holding up one kilo, I saw the reaction, the standing ovation! People clapping! – all directed towards him.

I just looked everywhere and said, "Wait a minute, I guided him. I set the whole thing up." It's bullshit.

Anyway, here's what we had to do. I couldn't leave. Kim and I were not allowed to leave Arizona until the judge signed me off on my charge, on my forgery of thirty Percocet.

I asked, "What do I do? Where do I go?"

"Go hide somewhere," says the captain. "Just go and hunker down. We'll get back to you as fast as we can."

Kim and I took off. We found a town- Wilcox, right on the edge of Arizona. We had to pay for our motel room and our food and we had no idea how long we were going to stay there. They had one diner in town, a truck stop. At first, I was upbeat about their buffet of BBQ ribs and chicken. The first night it smelled great and I went in and loaded a plate up. Kim enjoyed it. But after the second night, the third night, fourth night it got old. To this day I can't eat ribs and I can't eat too much chicken. We got so damn sick of ribs and chicken. That's all that was in that town.

Now just imagine being stuck on the border of Arizona with a fucking drug cartel after you or what was left of it. You knew there could be people out there hunting you and they were not going to be pleasant. If they found us, we were dead. There was a movie store right beside us where you could rent movies and that was our fun. Every day we would go over and rent six, eight, or ten movies. We had a little VCR in our room so we watched movies. And we did have a lot of sex, a lot of sex. We were trapped together. It actually brought us closer.

Now me with my addiction, I always had some pills in my pocket, always. That's sad. But I was running out. There were two doctors in Wilcox so sooner or later I hit both of them up using my salesmanship. With those injuries from my back, I got some Lorcets and Vicodin. One doctor gave me twenty-four Lorcets and another gave me forty Vicodin. That was a very apprehensive time of our life, just waiting. The days were going by so slow.

All I wanted was to get home and get my life straightened out. I mainly wanted to feel normal-to get over that mountain, this time to do it right, to finally just be free of this addiction. I was so tired of being a slave with the anxiety, the constant stress, and the pain that is there for weeks and weeks. You think it is never going to go away. Don't let anyone fool you. Opioid withdrawal is one of the worst withdrawals you can go through. Even after the physical effects are gone, which is about two to three weeks, maybe four, the mental effects last on and on and on. Every time I'd wake up, I would pray that this curse would be lifted from me.

I'd lie there looking around thinking, *Could this be the day?*

Ladies and gentlemen, this disease is totally evil. That's why people cannot get clean and stay clean. We are not bad people trying to get good. We are sick people trying to get well. And back then we didn't understand just how long the mental part of it was, just how devastating it was. It was so hard to put it into words. But imagine waking up every day of your life with this crushing headache. Now if you don't think, if you don't move, if you stare at a TV like a zombie, you're ok. But your brain is broken. As soon as you try to talk, as soon as you try to think, *Oww!* There's that terrible feeling like a gum-band being stretched across the front of your head. You're so sick, so nauseated and stressed. The stress and anxiety are unbelievable.

The depression Is like no other. You see even when you're in a mode of depression naturally, your endorphins still work, just not as many and they're not kicking as high as they should. But once you get addicted to opioids and they are taken away from you, your endorphins do not work at all. They are dead for a while. It's like not using your arm for a year in a cast, taking the cast off. You can't do a freakin' thing with that arm until you build it back up. And that takes months! Well, the same thing with your endorphins. So when you have no endorphins whatsoever, you go to the depths of depression that cannot be described. It can't be put into words very easily and that's what I want to do. You think of negative things. You think of the worst things that can happen to you. You have the gloomiest outlook on life and everything is sheer negativity, sheer drudgery, sheer evil. I mean it's like just going down, down, down. That's why there are so many suicides. And the reasons for the suicides are not explained well.

The reasons for a lot of suicides in opioid addicts is because they're not handling withdrawal correctly. You need to be around people. You need to be around someone that knows what you're going through. You need to get moving with physical activity. Try to find things you enjoy and make yourself move. Make yourself do things that hurt so bad, but every day you're working to get better. Now this takes months. Here is the kicker. Through the worst parts of withdrawal, you know a couple pills would give you relief. Now imagine three, four, or five weeks of sheer pain, sheer anxiety, sheer stress, depression, and you know that if you take a couple of pills, you can have about four, five, six hours of relief. OI. life is good. Oh... I feel great for a while. And believe me, that is why people cannot get over to the other side of the mountain. If you are into withdrawal four, five, or six weeks and you grab some pills and you take them, all that pain and suffering was for nothing. You may as well start over. Your brain goes right back to where it started from. It's called "progression." It is the most terrible feeling in the world to know if you slip up once to try to get just a little bit of freedom, a little bit of relief- all that suffering, all that pain was for nothing!

Therefore, once you take some pills, you are off to the races. You are addicted again! Life on life's terms, it's the most evil drug in the world. And it will take all that is good out of you. It will sap your soul right out of you. All that is good in your life is gone. All your love is gone. The only thing you love now is getting those opioids into your system to feel well. Because after you have been addicted for a while, you don't get high. You do not get that buzz. You are just trying to feel well so you can live a kind of normal life. As you become immune to a certain dose, you must take more to cope. All those pills contain high doses of acetaminophen. one Lori-set would contain 10 mg. of Hydrocodone and 750 mg. of acetaminophen or Tylenol. That right there is what destroys your liver. OK, just ten pills per day would be 7,500 mg. of Tylenol. Wow! Then combine that with drinking alcohol.

Every day in Wilcox, I would look behind me and all around for the cartel's revenge. Kim was a bundle of nerves. Well, the day came. I got the phone call. This was after thirty-three days in Wilcox, Arizona eating fucking ribs and chicken and watching movies over and over again. We drove back into Tucson. We were so grateful leaving Wilcox, Arizona. That was the most nerve wracking thirty-three days of my life.

We sat in front of a judge. I was given a public defender. The judge could not believe what he was hearing.

He looked at me and said, "Why the hell are you still here?"

I said, "Your honor, we were made to stay here until you signed us off."

He looked over at somebody at the side of the court and said, "This is bullshit. This should've never happened." The judge was pissed.

He looked at me and said, "Mr. Weaver, I am so sorry. When they busted this cartel, they got so many people in the cartel "snitching" to try to get themselves out of trouble that it just became a quagmire of new busts and new leads. You have no idea what you started, son. You have started the bust up of Nogales being the biggest importer of cocaine. Hell, we didn't even have guards stationed to get into Nogales. Nobody would stop you. You could just take that highway and drive right into Nogales and right out. When they did have guards at the gate, they were being paid off. This is all changing because of you, Mr. Weaver."

Here are his words exactly. "Looking at this charge, this is a pretty big charge. You did forge a prescription. It's a third-degree felony son. But on behalf of what you did for our state and the country, you may leave. But I want you to get clean and I want you to stay clean. So I am not dismissing the charges. I am setting them back and I am leaving them here. If I ever hear of you getting in trouble again, if you're ever in Tucson and you get in trouble son, these charges will be kicked back out."

I'm standing there thinking, *Oh my God, alright judge, just let me go. I'll be a good boy. I just wanted out of Tucson so fucking bad.*

Now before I was let go, the district attorney came up to me and said, "Son, you violated five years of probation in Oakland, Maryland and you have charges on you in Blair County, Pennsylvania. You didn't negotiate these well. You should've had a lawyer before you made this huge bust. You should've had a lawyer standing right there negotiating for you. You could've got out of everything plus you probably could've made out like a bandit."

He said, "On the average, anyone that brings us a kilo of cocaine is paid a couple thousand dollars for it. Now we couldn't have done that in your case. You would've been a multimillionaire. But we could've actually given you enough that you would've been well off. What you did for us would've set you up for a long time. But that little charge screwed everything all up. And you not getting a lawyer also was bad."

"Oh my God, who the hell can think of all these specifics during the busting of a drug cartel," I sighed.

But anyways the judge was great. I thanked him. He wished he could've done more for me.

All he said was, "Godspeed Mr. Weaver. From seeing what you did for us, I'm sure you're going to do more good for this country. If I can ever be of service again, call my office."

I'm hearing this from a judge. This made me feel great. My self-esteem was growing!

Well, this is what I found out on the way home when I called my dad as Kim and I were driving back. Sonny, the chief sergeant of Blair County Task Force told my dad to tell me to report a week after I got home. I knew exactly what that son of a bitch wanted. He wasn't going to let me go. Judge Thayer wanted to see me in Oakland, Maryland with my attorney. What the hell was going on? I was burned out. I was drained. I was eating my damn pills. The five-day ride home was very, very quiet and uneventful. And I had thought I could hold my head high and be proud.

Life sometimes is not good. I knew what was coming. I was just tired of all this, so burned out. And I was not going to be allowed to get clean. Dammit. I knew it. You cannot go into this world of drugs and people doing illegal activities and stay clean. It's impossible. That's why the police can't make too many busts. The only way to get trusted by people that are buying and selling drugs is to do drugs with them, to take them. And cops aren't allowed to do it. That's why they rely on "snitches" or undercover informants, as they call them. Let us do the dirty work for them. It's not right.

Kim and I made it home. I am back in my $30,000 home in Newry, PA which I owned. It was like a big circle. Here I was. I felt like a rabbit right back where I started -with the raid at my house, totally set up by the police. The man that brought the pot and the man who took the pot were both "snitches." What the hell did the district attorney want from me? All they said was to come in and talk. Didn't I do enough? How could they charge me for this "entrapment" after I did what I did in Tucson, Arizona? Life isn't fair, especially when you are stereotyped as a low-life drug addict.

CHAPTER 7

NO WAY OUT! TRAPPED IN MY HELL ON EARTH.

This was life changing, total life changing. Monday morning comes and I go to headquarters and there is Sonny Burner, chief lieutenant and his gang from the Blair County narcotics division. I was tired. I was burned out. The last two years of my life were like a movie.

"You did one hell of a job out there," says Sonny.

They all shook my hand.

"Congratulations, but you didn't do anything for us, nothing for Blair County."

My heart dropped. Come on. I saved thousands of lives. I did what most men couldn't do. Yet they wanted more. They weren't going to let me go.

You see, I thought that bust out in Tucson, Arizona was going to make national news. It was the fourth largest bust in the southwestern United States of America. I actually thought I was going to be congratulated by a lot of people. And I thought my days were over of running and hiding. But no. And I was so sick and tired of no one knowing of that bust out there. I initiated everything. It came out so well; it was dangerous. But because I had that third degree felony forgery charge, even though I was sick going through withdrawal, they covered it all up. And they were not going to put it out in the newspapers. They wanted to go get more people. All those people they caught in Tucson and Nogales were snitching. So I basically opened them up to a vast, vast area of drugs and cartels.

Here we go. I'm getting screwed. You see, Sonny and all these other people at the Blair County narcotics division do not give a shit about addiction, about ruining people's lives. All they're thinking about is their glory, their jobs, their big busts. It's true! The medical field finally has established over the years that opioid addiction is a disease. Once addicted, you are sick trying to get well! But in law enforcement, you still have those ignorant, self-serving lawmen who say you are a bad person trying to get good. Law enforcement seems to feed off drug addicted people when they open up a new agenda where they can sway sick and suffering addicts to work for them as "confidential informants" or snitches. This is a direct route into the drug world! – a road too hard for them to follow due to rules and regulations. They get the glory while the addicts risk their lives and health working for them. This is very unfair and dangerous for the addicted person!

So here's where my life takes a terrible turn. I can remember at that time thinking, *OK, I can become an undercover cop and do more good for everyone*. In my mind, I was justifying and twisting everything I had to do. It's so sick. I was thinking I can still party. I have an excuse to keep taking the life sapping chemicals because I'm helping people!

I asked Sonny, "You know I have to act normal and party with these people."

His exact words, "We don't want to know anything you have to do! Just bust people!" See! Just make us look good. It's all a testosterone driven contest.

You see, the only way to get clean and stay clean is to totally separate from people, places, and things having anything to do with drugs! You can get killed by being discovered or overdose by using and ruin years of your life staying sick just to make the law enforcement agents look good! To be an informant you must live and participate in the drug world!

By the way, Sonny was a functioning alcoholic. Every day after work you'd find him up at a bar near Ashville, Pennsylvania. It was known everywhere, but he did his job and he was pretty good at it.

"But I was entrapped," I said to Sonny, "I could've fought this. The guy that bought the marijuana was working for you and the guy that took the marijuana was working for you."

"Oh, yes Craig, but you were a willing participant. As long as you go along with it, you're guilty."

"How many more people did you do this to, Sonny? How many more sick and suffering son of a bitches did you take down just to get your glory, just to get your bust?' That pissed me off to no end.

"Screw the lives of people that are addicted, trying to get better, and got caught up in this whole situation because they turned into animals. It is a disease. You are not bad trying to get good. You are sick trying to get well. It hits doctors, it hits lawyers, it hits all walks of life, Sonny."

I called them all bastards.

I'm thirty-four years old, back in my house in Newry and I thought I would be able to start a new life.

"But you want six months of me being a snitch in my hometown, in my area?"

"Yes, we do," says Sonny. "You have to do something for us. You can do it, Craig. We have faith in you."

Well, ladies and gentlemen, you know what this means. I'm never going to get off these opioids. I wanted so bad to get better. I didn't care if it took two months, three months, a half a year. Once you become a snitch or as I thought about it an "undercover cop"- it's back to the movies. And that's what I put my mindset to.

"Are we going to make another movie or is my movie still going on?" I thought. I'm still the main actor and they just hired me to be an undercover cop.

So you see, what I did ladies and gentlemen, I did not go after my friends, people I knew, people I associated with. That would've been easy prey and that would've ruined me in this area for life.

What I did was I literally became an undercover cop. I went out and I met people. I met them in the drug world. I knew where to go. I knew how to act and what to do. I decided to go for it. I had to use my God given talent to guide me. Then I still had to do six months of work release in jail. That was the deal. I blew it by fleeing the area from prosecution. They had me good. They had more charges on me than just the pot. Fleeing prosecution is a crime in itself- five years minimum mandatory.

So let's go. I was disgusted. I started my food delivery service back, kept the $40,000 plus in jewelry, which was now about $60-70,000. I gave mom the store in Altoona. I basically started over again with the jewelry. You see, I had thousands of customers that were buying from their houses. I had people doing jewelry parties and jewelry shows. They were all so glad to see me back. I forget the excuse I told them. But I gave them a good excuse of why I disappeared for two years. Miraculously they all took me back. They all started buying food and jewelry from me.

Now I had one more problem to deal with before I could get going. five years of probation in Oakland, Maryland from my cocaine deal was violated. I was supposed to do five years in jail for violation of probation. So here comes Richard P. Brickens, my attorney- $5,000 for him to meet me in Oakland, Maryland. But the great thing is he was well informed of my bust in Arizona. The day of my hearing in Oakland, Maryland, he walks right in to the judge's chambers, very bold move, - never even talked to the DA. He walked right in to Judge Thayer's office, sat down, and told Judge Thayer exactly what happened.

So, I go in the court. The DA doesn't know what to do.

My attorney just said, "Okay judge, you're on."

Judge Thayer looks at him, looks at me and says, "We're going to let Craig go. We're dropping these charges. What Mr. Weaver did out in Arizona was amazing. He risked his life. I think this outweighs his past dealings. So, Mr. Weaver, you are free to go."

Now you would think that the DA would be pissed and the other cops that made the bust in Deep Creek, Oakland, Maryland would be mad. But I'll never forget this. After the hearing, I walked out into the hallway and it's guarded. The DA comes up to me, shakes my hand; the police came up to me, shake my hand.

Judge Thayer comes up to me. "Craig, you can't come to my house anymore and sell me food. It just wouldn't be right but you did one hell of a job, young man. Don't stop. Keep going. Do good."

I really liked Judge Thayer. He was a tough old geezer. He sucked at playing the bagpipes. I didn't like his Scotch but I loved the man, a good man.

Well, ladies and gentlemen, here we go. I started my food delivery service and jewelry and went back to Oakland, Maryland. I got all my customers back...Clearfield, State College, PA., Philipsburg, PA, Harrisburg, Pittsburgh and I was on a roll. But at the same time, I had to make busts for the Blair County task force.

There is a culture of people in every community living below well, hiding in their homes, in the back streets and alleys-giving up hope...zombies, dark hollow eyes. Maybe indirectly I could help these people. Think about this. They would do that for the rest of their lives, most of them. They have given up hope. We call them paycheck junkies. They get their welfare checks and for two weeks they can supply enough opioids for themselves. They sell a few here and there, buy a few here and there. But then there's two weeks that they're waiting for that check and they're sick. They're below well.

You always run out, ladies and gentlemen. You always run out.

Herein lies the old saying, "One is too many and a thousand is not enough." That sickness is disgusting. So what I figured is I would go into these places and I would hook up with people that were buying and selling drugs, mainly opioids, and I would set them up. And I didn't actually do it to be evil, to be bad. Going to jail for an opioid addict is a good thing. They know how to deal with them in jail. It gets you clean. If you get a three-month sentence, you come walking out of that jail feeling better and liking yourself again. And some people can start a new life.

That's the first step. You must get clean. That was my thinking. So many people were dying from this disease. Oh, I can remember going into these apartments that were filthy, junk heaped up, kids running around with no clothes on, dirty needles everywhere on the floor. And I would have to sit in there for hours waiting for a hookup. If they said they could get you some pills and they would have them in an hour, that usually meant four hours, six hours, eight hours. Sometimes they never came through. There is no honor among opioid drug addicts that are very sick, no honor at all. Some people took the money and never came back to their own apartment until I left. I mean it was just terrible but I did it. Hell on earth.

I became a damn good undercover cop, and in six months, I made seventeen busts. Oh, the stories I could tell. I was amped up from my role as an undercover cop. It was a means to an end. I did a good job. I did not bust anyone I knew or any friends. But once you're in the game, you have to use, partake. It's so sad. I was clean when I came home from Arizona. Now I'm back, I'm addicted again. Buying pills, selling pills, setting people up- it is a hard job to do one drug bust. The cops have to be coordinated. You have to plan the timing. You're not on the police's schedule or their time clock; you're on the damn addict's time clock or the druggies' time clock, the people that you're trying to bust. And they don't give two shits about time. They don't care about anything except what they get in their bodies. The biggest bust I made was an ounce of cocaine.

Mostly I ran around making little busts, thirty pills- Percocet, Lorisets, some pot. But I had to party and play the role. I had to take more drugs.

And I also had to run two businesses. The jewelry business was taking off. The steak and seafood business was doing well. And I actually built my businesses back up the same time I was working for the police. The only problem is my addiction was growing. I was becoming immune and I needed more and more every day. My addiction was heading to the limits of my destruction, my demise.

I'm in my middle thirties now. Kim is still with me. She knew what I was doing. She would give me a hand once in a while. She actually went to work for my mother at her jewelry store that I gave her. So I had all the elites, the wealthy class, the upper middle class, in eight or nine cities, not only buying tons of food every month, but also great amounts of jewelry. I was giving them a good product at half the price -at least, of any store. I was having trouble maintaining my addiction and there were times when I'd run out. But I had so many connections now, so many people, I could usually come up with something. I was dancing with the elites and running with the junkyard dogs. My life was full. I was known as "the Jewelry Dude" to the drug world.

What sucks is I had the ability to become friends with both groups of people- the elites and the junkyard dogs. I knew how to read them and get along with them. I was good at it. I met so many doctors selling food and jewelry to them. I remember three or four doctors in State College would combine and buy these buildings and all total had about twelve to fifteen nurses working for them. I had one place where I would bring a jewelry display in and lay it out in their break room. All the nurses and doctors would be buying.

Now I became friends with a bunch of the nurses and had a few affairs with them. What I had going, under the radar, was not only were the doctors giving me Percocet prescriptions, but I had four nurses, at the same time, trading me pills for jewelry, pills for food. And they did not know each other was doing it for me. You see, in all these places, all these medical facilities, they had a sample room. And drug companies would just send them thousands of samples- Vicodin, Loroset. The Loroset 10s were really powerful - 10mg of Hydrocodone and 650mg of acetaminophen. You throw five to six of them in your mouth and you're good for five to six hours. What was killing me was the acetaminophen. I was eating 20-30,000 mg. per day. It wasn't the good shit that was killing me. It was the acetaminophen destroying my organs, especially my liver. I went from six pills a day to ten to fourteen. But somehow, I kept handling everything. How the hell did I do all that. Not only was I physically addicted, but mentally I was so deep.

I worked for the Blair County task force for about six months. I made seventeen busts and somehow managed to keep my other life together. Oh, the stories I could tell doing those busts. It was so sick and twisted enough to write a book. The worst thing about this is my addiction grew and grew and grew. I needed a regimen every single day and was acutely addicted. I was dying. Now remember I still had six months of work release to do. Since I made all these busts around Blair County, the DA moved my jail time over to Bedford County. I only had six weeks before I went to jail.

And I decided to go to a rehab so I could deal with prison better. Here we go again. You see, the rehab is the easy part. You're supervised and monitored. You just deal with the pain and they help you a little bit. The main problem is once you leave that rehab, you still have the cravings. You are still an addict. Your brain is still twisted. You must keep so busy and fight this disease every day by hanging around people that are clean, people that are not addicts. You can't go into bars. You can't. You have to change your life entirely. And if you take one pill, one opioid, it's back to the races, -you are addicted again. There were times, ladies and gentlemen, when I would take one pill and not touch another one for a week. "Oh, I'm fine. You see, I'm cured." But then in another week I'd take two to three pills and in four days, I'd take some more pills. And in two days, I'd take some more. Sometimes it took me six months to get addicted again. But dammit once I took that first pill after I got clean, once I opened that door, you might as well hand everything over that you've done, because you are going to lose everything that you have gained. It is going to be taken away from you.

Remember this disease wants us dead. It's still only 10-12% recovery rate and I know why. It's the six months after the damn rehab. Everyone thinks they're cured, that they can handle it and they can do it. But you are not cured. Like I said, it's the only disease that you will lie to yourself. Subconsciously your body and your mind will tell you that you're fine, that you're ok, but you're not. Once you become an addict it changes the way your brain works and changes the way you think. There are three things that you subconsciously don't have to think about, but you do them every day. You need food, you need clothing, and you need shelter. Those three things you just have to do and you don't even have to say it out loud.-. "Oh, I have to eat today" or "I must find warmth." No, once you become an opioid addict, that compartment has a fourth item in it. Your subconscious mind thinks you need food, clothing, shelter and opioids. It rewires itself. That's why you always have cravings, you always desire that high. You are never cured. You always have this disease waiting in the wings, preying and hoping that you will screw up.

I went to Cove Forge. I can remember talking to therapists at Cove Forge about certain situations in my life. But not one of them touched the surface or dug even a third deep enough to address my deep-rooted life altering events. You see, this is the problem. They don't go deep enough.

"What caused you to have OCD? What were the tragic events in your life whether it's superficial, whether it is something about you, whether you have a deformity?"

There always is a deep-rooted problem that was never addressed in your youth like family dysfunction. Anything that you think about 24/7 that you can't get out of your head and bothers you constantly will manifest itself if it's not dealt with. It will either come out as a disease or a sickness or you will develop obsessive compulsive disorder. I see it so clearly and obviously now.

Anything I found that would take my mind off of my problems, I would obsess in. I'll still kick anyone's butt in shooting pool. That was the first thing that I could get out of my head with. And I got so good. You see, a lot of people obsess in something that will treat them great in life. They obsess in something and become great at it like playing the guitar or excelling at a trade and they're lucky. With me, I was obsessing in pool, hunting and fishing, and other things like sex.

Lo and behold, when my femur got busted and I found this world of opioids would take me out of any bad situations that I was compelled to think about all day, I was gone. If I wouldn't have busted my femur, I wouldn't be writing this book right now. My goal was to be an entertainer, a radio or TV broadcaster, a singer, an actor. I loved the arts. I loved doing things like that even though all through my teen years I was told to stay away.

"Very few people make it," mom would say.

Well, here I am, and you know what, I'm still going to do it. At age sixty-two, I'm still going to succeed. It's like my brain stopped at age nineteen, but now I'm jumping into these desires I had that would've aspired me to new heights of greatness. After nine years of being clean, I'm doing all those things over again. I grabbed the guitar and have been doing speaking engagements and have a comedy routine. It's like I'm back to where I stopped at age nineteen.

So, I got out of the rehab. I was as ready as I will ever be for the six months of work release. Oh, I was still nervous. I was still scared. You go there hoping to start work release right away but it's all up to the lieutenant running the jail system.

Now here's the first big problem. I'm thrown in a cell with a disgusting person and the lieutenants decide to wait thirty days before I could start work release.

"Let him sit here for thirty days just to punish him a little bit."

I was put in a cell with a twenty-year-old West Virginia hillbilly. This kid was out of control and was a complete animal, a complete lunatic. He made my life a living hell. Thank God I was clean or I would've killed him. But as it would happen, he was dirty; he was crude. He would be jacking off in the cell on his bed all day long just doing disgusting things over there. He couldn't even wait till night.

Oh, I would yell at him, "Leave that thing alone."

He never washed. This was weighing on me every day. Disgusting things. I could hardly eat food around him. But we were in together twenty-three hours a day. We got out one hour to shower. Well, one day it happened. We get our lunch trays at noon. He gets his and he sits on the toilet. This West Virginia hillbilly takes a shit while he's eating his lunch and I'm trying to eat mine. And I can hear him and I can smell it. That's it. I lost it. I went over and right on the toilet, I slapped him. I gave him a backhand so hard, he flew off the toilet, food flew everywhere. The guards came. Here we go. I kind of whacked him a little too hard and his eye turned black. I had him in a full Nelson when the guards came and it didn't look good. I wouldn't have killed him but I wanted to hurt him. I had had enough and he needed put in his place and to learn a few manners.

Now this is the old Bedford County Jail where they had a basement and you're still allowed to smoke back then. The next thing I know, I'm thrown in the basement. OK. Who else is in the basement? The worst of the worst of the worst-the child molesters, the rapists, the murderers. You see, this is right off the Pennsylvania turnpike. You would have outsiders just getting pulled over and they'd find bad things happening like fugitives running from the law and they'd get caught. So you had thirty-five to forty people down in this dungeon as I called it. Instead of two to a cell, there were four to a cell. And they would open the cells up in the morning and you had five or six picnic tables. There was no ventilation, no windows and everyone smoked. So, I'm down there with these disgusting dangerous criminals and had to spend three weeks with them. Oh my God.

I finally found someone that I could relate to and we hung together. But it was the worst three weeks of my life. Every day went so slow. I would stand with my back against the wall. You couldn't go in your cell because three other guys were in there most of the time. I couldn't sleep. And after a while I'd quit asking people what they were in there for. Of course, they were all innocent. But I found out, I was in there with some pretty dangerous people, actually very dangerous people. The cigarette smoke was horrific. You could not see ten feet in front of you. Fights broke out every day. Just the crazy look they would give you and the wild thoughts they were thinking, so sick and twisted, mentally tormented me. But I made it!

I finally got my work release, once again connected with all my customers. I had to come up with another excuse why I left for four weeks. These people were great to me. I just love all of them. They were so faithful and stuck by me. And I think most of them knew what was going on, that I had some pretty major issues. But they saw me becoming a success throughout all this crap, all this demented shit I had to endure during this disease. I was still making it. Somehow, I put everything together; these businesses were snowballing! I was becoming the American Dream. Lord help me, I was so sick.

Don't tell me why, but for some reason, the best food on the planet and great quality jewelry went together- especially bringing it to peoples' houses.

"First, I want this in food and then bring in your jewelry display and I want this and this and this."

I was walking out of houses with $1,000, $2,000. I would go to Oakland, Maryland with these rich coal company owners and would come back with $10,000 in my pocket. And then they started doing jewelry shows. Incredible. I sit here right now and my chest just got tight just knowing what I built up, just knowing how hard I worked, just knowing what I did. I was good to these customers.

There is no one that worked harder than me. I worked sick. I worked through withdrawal. I would always make my deliveries and my logistics had to be dead on. I had to be in State College at 12 sometimes and then Clearfield by 2:30 and Philipsburg by 4. And then buy jewelry and food for the next day to start at 5 AM. Amazing.

And I threw it all away. I had to get rid of everything to save myself, which you are going to read in the next few chapters...how close I was to death, where it led me. So, get ready, it doesn't get any nicer. But it's the truth, ladies and gentlemen. We need to know the truth. We need to know where this disease will take us. Nobody wants to go there. Everyone has a story. Some stories must be told and this is one of them. Because I'm still alive. And there's no way I should be alive. I love life. I love every moment of it. I could sit in a damn yard staring out in the woods and enjoy myself. Life is precious. It goes by quick. If this book saves one person or helps one person, then I have done my job. For what better gift can you give to humanity than the gift of life. I'm a driven man now. I can't help it. I shouldn't be here.

OK, I'm done with work release, done with Sonny Burner, all the cops. One big thing that happened during work release was Kim got pregnant. It wasn't all work. They had no clue where I was during the day, where I was going, what I did. I just had to show them receipts. So our first child was on its way and I was glad. I figured this was karma and I could now settle down and live right.

So, back in those days, when somebody gets somebody pregnant and you're together, you usually get married. So Kim and I got married. We got married at a place called Swallow Falls – about a sixty-foot-high waterfall-in Deep Creek Lake, Oakland, Maryland. One of my food customers, Butch, who I partied with down there, could marry people. He had a license. So one day we take off, sell food and jewelry, then get married that evening. At Swallow Falls while the sun was setting- we were standing on a rock at the top of the waterfalls. It was beautiful. Kim and I had some amazing times and that was one of them. It was just like the night in San Francisco.

So now Kim's working for my mother and I'm released from jail. Needless to say, my businesses are snowballing. Work release was the one time in my life that I could take off with my businesses. They actually grew tenfold in those six months. Work and sleep. Work and sleep. And boy did I work. I was clean. Things were going amazing.

But If I remember correctly, I had a couple teeth pulled and got a script for ten Percocet. I deserved these. This is different. I'm in pain. The door was opened. The monkey jumped back on my back. I knew how to handle it. I was pretty used to it. The main thing I remember is the jewelry business growing out of control; people were starting to buy $10,000 items, $20,000 items. My reputation was impeccable for jewelry-and food. I became so close to Dave, the owner of Precious Metals and Diamonds Company and was over there all the time. I started making $30,000, $40,000 buys and signing for it. He gave me a $100,000 credit limit. And for the jewelry shows, I could still load up on consignment items and it looked like a five-million-dollar display.

The crazy thing is that with my steak and seafood customers and business combined with the jewelry I was throwing all my money into paying the jewelry off. I would pay a $30,000 jewelry bill in three months. And I'd buy more. I can remember, in my mind's eye, thinking I must get all the jewelry I can, acquire as much as I can get. And own it, pay for it. Then I can retire with a huge jewelry store and every sale I make would be total profit. And give it to my kids when I pass on. That was my mindset. It was so wrong, if only I would've started investing a little bit.

Jewelry is not an investment. But me and my warped sense of thinking from the disease and OCD obsessed in jewelry. That was what I was doing. I obsessed in it. My display grew and grew. I started needing three jewelry cases to carry around, I mean those big suitcase looking cases, then four, then five. My jewelry shows were taking off. I was doing them at country clubs, at wealthy houses, at bars, anywhere, and they were all growing.

We had our son Lisle. And Kim decided the house wasn't big enough or nice enough to raise a family in. I even let her brother who was a carpenter put an addition on. It was $17,000 and a kind of a different addition – one huge room that went out onto a deck straight into a swimming pool with sliding glass doors. Now in that room was my bed, a beautiful bar, and a pool table. That was my quarters, my pleasure room, as you might call it. And it was absolutely beautiful. I could get out of bed, run out and jump in the swimming pool, mix a drink and shoot pool.

Before I married to Kim, so many things happened in that room. Not only was I good at selling, I became good at picking up women and picked up many. When you're addicted, your sexual desires become different, kind of like just warped. Instead of the normal way to do things, you just get into another level. Your fantasies are twisted a little bit. I got into bondage and playing games, things like that. I'm not going to say it wasn't exciting because I did have some good times with the wrong women. I picked up a lot of dancers and one stayed with me for the longest time. I tried to get her out of my house.

She sat in the middle of the highway yelling, "I am going to let a car run me over if you kick me out."

Crazy times. She didn't get hit by a car. "Foxy Roxy" was her dance name.

That's before Kim and I got tight, before she moved in, before Lisle was born. But Kim was with my mom 97% of the time. And I was just on my own.

When you become addicted, everything changes. You think differently. You act differently. You are not the same person. All that is good will definitely sooner or later be taken away from you-your ability to love, your compassion, your empathy. You don't care about a damn thing except what you are addicted to. That is your true love.

Everything else is secondary. Just like carrying $10,000 in my pocket after a hard day's work in Oakland, Maryland-it was nothing to me, it was not exciting. I did not treat it like I should've. I just couldn't wait to enjoy my evening.

See, that's where my childhood comes in. I could not think two weeks ahead, a month ahead. I was still in the mindset from my youth, of thinking for the evening, of having just a good day, a small reward system, whether it is getting laid, whether it is going out to a nightclub, whether it is cooking crab legs and filet mignon. That's all I thought about at the time was enjoying the day. It all comes together now. When we were kids, we couldn't think of the future. We just prayed that our parents wouldn't fight that night and we could have an easy-going evening, one where we wouldn't be on edge and our nerves would be a wreck. That was our mindset. I could write a whole other book about the sick world I went into and the things I did. But I want this book to be uplifting and the good side of me. When you're in the thralls of addiction, there is no good side to you. You lose it. You fake it. Most people can't tell.

You have one hell of a personality because your endorphins are dancing a thousand times more than they should be from your pills. But take those pills away, and you're done. Your life stops. Once withdrawal starts, you can't function. Try thinking of that every day. Try waking up knowing that if you run out of your drug, your whole world stops and all those in your world. I had so much going on. I was becoming wealthy, had a son, and a girl that would've been faithful to me for the rest of my life. I was making tons of money, had thousands of customers that loved me and I loved them. Talk about the American dream. But all I cared about while this was going on was getting high, staying high, not getting sick. No wonder there are so many suicides in drug addiction.

OK, so Kim and I are married and have a son Lisle. Like I said she thought that house was too small in Newry. I owned it and loved it there but for Kim and Lisle, I put it up for sale, got $40,000 for it. Kim used to work at Beneficial Finance and was very close with them and my sister's husband was a real estate agent. I called him to help my sister out. He sent me to a house in Sylvan Hills that I loved and I got it for around $100,000. Since Kim was still in good with Beneficial Finance, they mortgaged it for me. And I put $40,000 down on it, all the money I got for my house in Newry. So, I only owed $59,000 on it and my monthly payments were $1,250. It was a beautiful home in a nice ritzy area. It had a huge downstairs that was completely furnished. In the basement were twelve rooms that could store freezers; I put my warehouse in there. And my pool table was in another room. The family lived upstairs. Things were going well.

Of course, I was addicted to opioids again. I never had time to really get better. I needed at least three months, which I had no clue, to fight the cravings back after I got clean. Hell, if I left for three days, customers were calling and people were getting pissed off. I had too many responsibilities. So I just kept everything kicking to maintain my addiction. I would drive down to the backstreets of Altoona, get some pain pills. Or grab pain pills from my State College doctors or any other connections I had. I always managed to get pain pills, always managed to keep on keeping on. A lot of my money was going to pain pills. I was making too much. I was making more to overcompensate for those pills I had to buy and still moving ahead.

The jewelry shows were really taking off. Kim was with my mom constantly. A year went by. Kim and I started growing distant. She wouldn't get home till seven. I'd get home maybe 7:30-8. We were both so damn tired. No supper cooked. And I came home to a tired wife that wore this one pair of sweat pants, the most unsexy apparel you could wear. And we would just say a few words to each other. That was it. If you're in a relationship or you're married, I know sex isn't everything, but I do believe it's at least 30%. If you quit having sex, sooner or later, somebody's going to turn to alternate methods because we all need compassion, we all need to want somebody. We need physical touch.

So Kim and I were growing further and further apart. I started getting into pornography. There was a company in Chicago called "Leather and Lace" and I would buy videos every week. This company would let you write a script and for $500, they would make a movie out of it. And then you got a certain percentage of the sales that it made. So I did it. Pretty damn good movie if I do say so myself. I was into cat fights at the time, and like I said some bondage. I obsessed in it and that went on for a while. It's amazing as I sit here now, clean and sober for ten years, that I see just how addiction alters all thinking processes. I'm not a pervert or sadist at all. I love and respect women and am sometimes too much of a gentleman or should I say, too empathetic. During my addictive state, everything became darker and twisted! My brain could mainly just think of instant gratification for ME. Now I'm totally the opposite. I like to give. I enjoy helping and making people happy.

I've stated this many times, "Opioid addiction is the devil's tool. It's evil and will sap all the good out of a person and turn anyone into an animal."

Kim loved the jewelry store with mom and Lisle was doing fine. I was selling and selling and selling.

Then my jewelry shows started taking off in Altoona. I found a group of Italians, the Michaela's, a bunch of sisters that were well to do, that loved having jewelry shows. They had a long list of relatives who all had money.

I met Dorothy Michaela; her nickname was "Doll". And she had the first jewelry party. I noticed her coming on to me and just being really friendly and helping me.

And after the event took place, she spent some time with me and said, "I have eight other relatives that already asked me to have shows."

And I said, "Fine, let's do them together. You take me there and help me set up and I'll throw you a few bucks."

Well, we became a team. She was living with a state cop, a fire marshal. I swear the first three, four months, I had no ill intentions. I was not even thinking about sexual events with her. But we got to know each other really well. She would bring Tom, her boyfriend, over to me and Kim's house. We'd have dinner together. We all got to know each other so we were all friends. Then I noticed she would keep staring at me at these jewelry parties. She was getting closer to me and would call me. It had been about a year and a half since I had sex with a woman, especially my wife.

One night after a party, she came up to me. I think she was drunk. I'll never forget this.

"How about if I come over tomorrow afternoon and fuck your brains out," her exact quote. And I did not say "No."

Well, once the next day came, that's all it took. She was a medical secretary at the Altoona Hospital. Her boyfriend was fifteen years older than her. She was forty and he was fifty-five at the time and they hadn't been in any sexual relationship. She came over and we kinda crashed into each other. Then it started. We were in lust. She would get a half hour break for lunch at the hospital. I'd pull in the damn parking garage. She'd come down and we would have sex in my vehicle. We couldn't stay away from each other. One time she told her boyfriend that we were going to go fishing. She said she loved to fish and I was a fisherman. We were in the Holiday Inn at 6 AM, had a case of beer, spent the whole day together. We had feelings for each other; we developed them. But we had to keep the friendship going between all four of us.

Doll and I would see each other as much as possible and I kept everybody close.

I started singing with a band at a place called Altoona Tavern and I would sing every weekend. And Doll would be there. Kim wouldn't want to go. Those were some good days. Kim and I kept growing further apart but Kim and mom were happy and inseparable.

I went to Alaska with my dad and his two brothers, salmon fishing on the Kenai peninsula. I had just enough pain pills to take the ten-day trip. The trip was phenomenal. We travelled. We fished. We saw moose. We saw bear. It was the salmon capital of Alaska at the time. We went to Homer, Alaska, fourteen miles away- where they filmed "The Deadliest Catch." All those famous crab boats were docked there and we drank in "the Salty Dog."

When I came home, Kim and I had sex, the first time in a year and a half. She got pregnant with our daughter Kelcie, a blessing. One time, in a year and a half-it was amazing! So our second baby was on its way. All of a sudden, I had my little family – Lisle, Kelcie, me, and Kim.

Well, the affair with Doll got stronger and stronger. Everyone was getting suspicious. We would get motel rooms as often as possible. We obsessed in each other. One day I got caught. My dad came to the motel room in Ebensburg where we were at. I'm pretty sure Doll and I were in love then. We kept growing closer for months and months. I had a talk with my dad and I told him that I wasn't going to stop seeing Doll.

Here's a twist. I had a good friend named Steve. Here, I didn't know it but Kim was after Steve. They had eyes for each other six months before Doll and I ever had sex. So as soon as Doll and I were exposed, it wasn't three weeks until Kim and Steve were together. So what does that say. To be totally honest, she was looking for the same thing I was. I wasn't as bad as everybody thinks in that situation. There was nothing left with Kim and me. I, of course, was the bad guy! So many other circumstances led up to our divorce. One huge factor was the relationship between Kim and my mother. They were inseparable as I said. I'm positive their relationship was a main catalyst in not only our breakup but mom and dad's breakup after forty years of marriage. Also, we were turning into those couples you saw in the 1950s when one sat on a chair, the other sat on the couch, never talked, just bitch at each other. That's where we were heading.

The fire marshal was pissed at me. He threatened so many times to do me away-to kill me, to beat the shit out of me, which he knew he couldn't. Doll and I were inseparable.

Here's a strange way to live. My life was kicking. My businesses were kicking. And my addiction was kicking. I let Kim, Steve, and my kids live in my house in Sylvan Hills. Doll and I were living in a Holiday Inn. I came home every day and worked downstairs in my office with my freezers, running my businesses, seeing my kids. Kim and Steve lived upstairs. I paid all the bills for a year and a half- $3,000 a month is what everything came out to. Not only did I pay the bills for Kim, Steve, and the kids, I had to pay for the room at the Holiday Inn. I had to keep my businesses going, pay my own bills and keep my addiction going. Please, how did I do that. Oh my God. But I did it.

No wonder I burnt myself out. I was killing myself.

Then after selling tons of jewelry out at the Holiday Inn during the jewelry parties, running my steak and seafood business out of my house with Steve and everybody upstairs., Doll decides she wants to live in a house together. You see, Tom was only renting the house in Juniata, Pennsylvania where Doll and him lived. She had two boys. She talked Tom into moving and we took over the house in Juniata. So there I was, with a beautiful home in Sylvan Hills, living in a house in Juniata, running over to my home in Sylvan Hills and running my businesses. Crazy. Crazy. Crazy.

Now at this time I'm getting sicker and sicker. I'm taking more and more pills. Doll and I had a couple amazing years, -singing with the band, meeting drug friends there through the guys in the band, going to parties, working during the day. My growing businesses somehow kept everybody going. Making money and spending money and making money and spending money. Then Doll and I decided to break up. She was a cocaine addict. Things were getting bad. Too much was going on. I couldn't handle everything. So Kim and Steve and the kids find a new place in Hollidaysburg, an apartment. I move back into my house in Sylvan Hills. Doll's living in her place in Juniata. I decided to work out a figure with Kim and me for child support-$1,200 a month. So that's where everybody was after three to four years of chaos.

Somehow, I'm still afloat. Selling $10,000 diamonds, netted me $3-4,000. I was selling a lot of big-ticket jewelry and $900, $1,500 a day in food, still holding everything together but was getting sicker and sicker. Oh, I would try a rehab but couldn't stay for more than a week. Everything would've fallen. I was trapped in hell on earth.

One night I'm all alone in my big, big home in Sylvan Hills and there's a knock at the door. It's my dad.

"Mom kicked me out of the house, Craig. She found another man, the carpenter. I have nowhere to go, son."

"OK Dad, come on. Let's live together."

So, now it's me and Dad. Mom and the carpenter move in with each other. Kim and my kids are renting a house. Doll's in Juniata. I still have my jewelry business and food business kicking, somehow. My customers were so sincere about keeping me on and they were very faithful to me. They liked my product, they liked my pricing, and they liked me. My addiction was growing. I'm just hanging on physically.

Dad and I decide to go on a singles' cruise. Now at this time, I'm addicted, (Are you ready?) to twenty-four Vicodin a day. I was getting Vicodin 10s- twenty-four a day. No one can handle this. It's not the Hydrocodone, it's the acetaminophen. Each pill contains 650mg. And I'm taking twenty-four pills a day- six Vicodin every four hours. It nauseates you. So I'm on a cruise with my dad to the Caribbean. Oh, we had fun. We got off at the first stop, New Orleans, for the day. It was around noon when we go into a "house of ill repute" and grab two women. The next thing, Dad and I are in a room with each other, very weird. Two women naked, we're naked, very strange. Needless to say, with the amount of Vicodin in me and we were already drinking, I was not too potent in the sexual aspect. I could not perform as well as if I would've been clean and healthy. I had no problem even getting drunk as hell but with the combination of the pills, the alcohol, and being in the same room as my father – Hello! It wasn't working.

I'll never forget after that first drink in the bar in New Orleans, I couldn't recollect much more. In fact, Dad and I were out of it. We actually came to a conclusion they slipped us a "mickey. It was only noon but we were jumping from bar to bar. And I can't remember the rest of the damn day. All I know is we almost missed the ship. And that night on the ship after drinking all day and the Vicodin I had to take, I puked my guts out all night. I got sicker than a dog. Every time I would take a drink of alcohol, my liver would hurt. So with all this going on, I was destroying my body more than anything.

We get home from the cruise. My Dad was living with me. I was doing a ton of jewelry shows. One of my customers started helping me since Doll wasn't around. She was the accountant for W. S. Lee Food Distributors. She started having shows at her house once a week. She knew everyone in Altoona. Another lady who was the head nurse for a doctor in town also got interested and started having jewelry shows and helping me with jewelry parties. So I had two women that were very close to me that were watching me grow. They kept pushing me to start a jewelry store of my own again. Now remember, I had given my first store to my mom. Dad left her so it was "her baby." She was running it. But with my home delivery and jewelry parties, my display was growing by leaps and bounds and actually larger than hers. And it only took me a couple years. My nickname was "The Jewelry Dude." All my customers wanted me to put up a store. I had so much support from everybody. So many people, good honest citizens, who I called friends wanted me to succeed.

Now at the same time that I am living with my dad selling food and jewelry, trying to maintain my addiction, my disease was taking over. When you're up to twenty-four Vicodin a day, you can't maintain your health. I was drinking at all the jewelry parties/ jewelry shows. I was starting to get sick a lot and was losing weight. I was convening more with a certain group of people, Altoona's hard-core junkies-on 6th and 7th avenue, and these were the worst of the worst. They lived in row houses, crack houses. I got in with their crowd to get my opioids and started visiting that area three to four times a week. Some days I would spend the whole afternoon there. You see, what was starting to happen was that was my comfort zone. I was slowly but surely losing my faculties. I was turning into an animal. Not only was I physically getting sick but mentally, I was losing myself. Life was leaving me.

The things that were important I no longer cared about. You see, I had two kids, Lisle and Kelcie. This is so sad. I was doing good with having them over. At first after we split, they would be with me every other weekend. I was taking Lisle fishing and hunting, doing things with Kelcie. It was actually working. I was giving Kim $1,250 a month child support. But the sicker I got, the less I saw my kids. Subconsciously I didn't want my kids to go thru any dysfunction like I went thru. I kept that thought foremost in my head. Everything was still going OK with them; they were still young enough- seven and five. They couldn't see the internal structure or goings on and all the drama. All they saw was a dad that loved them and a mom that loved them and we were trying to keep things the best we could. So anyways, I wasn't seeing my kids often enough. I didn't want to hurt them mentally!

I was heading into the wrong side of town more frequently. I had doctors giving me pain pills but I needed more. My habit was becoming ridiculous. So with all this going on, I did jewelry shows at the Heidelberg Country Club and a country club in Oakland, Maryland. I was becoming known as the man to hire that had the best display. By this time, I had over a half a million dollars' worth of jewelry. I kept buying more and more on consignment but I was selling so much I could pay it off in two to three months. I was using money from my food business and big diamonds I'd sell. I'd make $5,000-$10,000 on one sale, a $30,000 diamond. But I threw it all into paying off my jewelry consignments. Therein lies my biggest screwup. I was into paying my jewelry off too much. I should've dished out the money in different areas, some towards my bills, some toward the steak and seafood company, some towards my jewelry stores, some towards ME, - a savings, an investment, a portfolio. I couldn't think like that. I was insane. I was growing more insane as the days went by. All I thought about, as things were growing quickly -was that reward system at the end of the damn day. Isn't that sad? It was getting laid; it was watching a freakin movie. That was all I could think about. I couldn't think of the future. I didn't give a shit about the future. I just figured it was the thing to do- to keep growing. I was high all the time. I worked high, I lived high 24/7. It was killing me.

CHAPTER 8
ENTER: HEROIN - NO MORE MAINTAINING

I had two fantastic customers named Jan and Dawn in State College- schoolteachers. They said they wanted to talk to me. We had become friends. They bought a lot of jewelry and food from me. Their dream in life was to have a gigantic building and use it for a store with everything -just one of those stores with all kinds of antiques and such. It just so happened this gigantic building came up for sale. It was the largest tallest biggest building in Tyrone, Pennsylvania. But it was too big for them, too much room, too much space. And it just so happened that Tyrone, Pennsylvania was the exact center of all my areas...Philipsburg, Clearfield, State College, Lewistown, and Oakland, Maryland. All these towns were around Tyrone and I-99 was the bypass that went right by Tyrone. Well, they called me up and we had a meeting. I decided to centralize my areas and put up a gigantic jewelry store. In fact, the ladies that were helping me- Patty and Sue, the accountant and the head nurse, were ecstatic.

"We will work for you. We will be so supportive. Put a store up."

Well, I went for it. I rented out the whole second floor of this gigantic building- a huge area. I hired a guy to be with me and help with everything and was paying him $400 a week to help carry food in, bring jewelry displays in, help me with jewelry shows. My dad also was helping me with buying jewelry cases and getting the building ready. I mean, I had one solid floor for silver and then a floor above it for the big stuff, the good stuff- 14k gold, diamonds, rubies, precious metals. That place was perfect. twelve jewelry cases it took just for the silver;

twelve jewelry cases just for the precious metals. I started telling people about it. It was a work in progress.

Now at the same time, I'm going into 6th and 7th Avenue and disappearing for half a day here, half a day there, buying pills, getting high. I was getting to know all these junkyard dogs and junkies. But I wouldn't try heroin. Heroin was a bad word. Even after taking all these pills and killing my damn organs, heroin to me was BAD.

The grand opening is only two weeks away, ladies and gentlemen. Everybody's involved, even my kids, my father, all the people that were close to me. I was having it catered-shrimp, crab legs, lobster and had people coming from West Virginia, Maryland, Pennsylvania. I had over a thousand people coming to this grand opening, all the best food customers, all my best friends, all my best people that had been with me throughout my business ventures, and my addiction. This was big.

At this time, I was having trouble maintaining my addiction. Opioids were becoming harder and harder to get. There were certain times that you couldn't get anything and you suffered. Plus, I was so into this grand opening, I didn't have time to look. As the days go by, I got all the jewelry cases in there and signed a lease. Everybody's excited. Not only did I have my whole jewelry display laid out, but I took a couple $100,000 worth on consignment from Precious Metals and Diamonds Company. The place looked like the best jewelry store ever! Some jewelry stores have been in business for 100 years but my place was nicer, better, and bigger.

This grand opening was going to show everybody that I had made it. Craig Weaver has made it! But underneath in my mind's eye, "I'm a piece of shit. I don't deserve this. I hope nobody finds out who I really am. I hope nobody really sees what I've become. I got to keep this secret world of mine hidden. I am a low life drug addict. I am no good." This is what goes through your mind at all times. Even though I worked my butt off, had a better work ethic than anyone I ever met- traveling the countryside and city, selling food, working fifteen to eighteen hours a day, buying jewelry, coding it...nonstop work, I didn't deserve any of it. How sad that is.

Well, the grand opening comes. My store is exquisite. It's 9 AM. I didn't have any pills. Nothing. I was too busy. Holy shit, I hadn't taken a pill since about midnight the night before. I was breaking out into sweats at 9 AM -in my tuxedo-as the caterer arrived. People weren't supposed to come until noon. I'm getting sicker and sicker and sicker. I started asking my friends who were close to me if they had any pills. I was frantic. By 11 AM, I was throwing up. My tux was soaking wet. I looked like hell.

People were saying to me, "What's wrong with you, Craig? You don't look good at all. Are you sick?"

People started coming in at noon. I couldn't even talk to them. I had a little office in the back and I'm sitting back there crying like a little baby. I made a phone call...6th Avenue, Altoona -an addict, a heroin addict.

"Help me, I said, "Get your ass over here."

Here comes this dirty kid, hadn't bathed in a week, smelled, disgusting who goes right up thru the damn jewelry store- "I-99 Antiques," it was called -and "Craig Weaver's Jewelry Store" -back into my office. He throws a bag of heroin on the table. I look at him. I'll never forget what he said to me.

"I'm going to make a man out of you today."

Isn't that sick? As I'm shaking, as I'm ready to have a heart attack- I'm thinking, *What the hell, I have to.*

I'm forty-two years old, the day of my grand opening - I-99 Antiques and Craig Weaver's Jewelry Store in Tyrone, Pennsylvania - 1,000 people coming... Craig Weaver snorts his first bag of heroin. It hit me like a ton of bricks. Son of a bitch, I felt great. I felt better than great. All my endorphins were just dancing. I was smiling, I was laughing, talking to everybody. I did $17,000 that day.

Now I want everyone that's reading this right now -to buckle up, get ready. Now, remember at age forty-two was my first bag of heroin. Where I'm about to take you, where my life heads to, where my life goes, is almost unthinkable. What that bag of heroin did to me, I can't put into words right now. Let's just say it was the beginning of the end for Craig Weaver. The store was kicking ass after that and I was a heroin addict. Two worlds were colliding!

Now snorting heroin, just snorting it, will get you high. But you lose a lot in your nose hairs and some comes back out. It takes a little longer to hit you. Two weeks after I snorted that bag, I wanted to shoot it. I wanted to feel the rush. I figured in my own mind, in my mind's eye, I might as well try it. I'm on heroin. I'm a curious son of a bitch.

The same guy that brought the bag that said he was going to make a man out of me at my grand opening was the man that showed me how to shoot dope. In his kitchen, I sat down. I was nervous. He takes the needle, poured the powder into a spoon, heated it up, threw some water in it, turned it into liquid, filled the syringe, found a vein in my arm, pulled the syringe back, drew blood.

Ladies and gentlemen, when that blood went back into my vein, I went for a ride, not of this planet. Euphoria covered my body like a blanket; I could feel it traveling all through me -just like warm water overcoming every part of my body. The first half hour, you don't want to move, you don't want to talk. You don't want to look at anything. You don't want to think about anything. I was out in my own world. Everything was perfect. This is what I always yearned for, I thought. This was the greatest feeling that ever came over me, my body. It was like an orgasm multiplied by 100 never ending. They call it "nodding" when you are in and out of consciousness, and you are just overtaken with warm, tingling beautiful thoughts and feelings.

Once I tried that first shot of heroin, not only did I fall in love with the feeling and effects, I fell in love with the whole ritual. I fell in love with filling that needle with heroin, finding a vein, and pulling that trigger back. And once that blood comes through that needle, it's pay time. You know that you are off to the races. You know you are going to be in a world unlike any other. And with my obsessive-compulsive disorder and with all the money I had, hell on earth was about to explode. I just fell in love, with the devil himself.

So here's where I am, here's what's going on... I borrowed $15,000 to start this store in I-99 Antiques. I had the whole second floor of this big building in Tyrone and had my two part time managers- two very influential women in Altoona-Patty, the accountant of W. S. Lee who quit her job and came with me and Sue, the head nurse for a doctor in Altoona. Sue worked with me anytime I wanted her. They were getting along great. They became friends and were bringing in customers right and left having jewelry parties. Patty was with the elites of Altoona. Sue was with the middle class and knew a lot of people, doctors especially who brought their wives.

I was shooting heroin and running my food business, still trying to keep that secret world hidden. But life was becoming hard. Every day

I needed a couple of bags of heroin. See, once you shoot heroin and you feel that euphoria, Percocet, Lorocet, and all the pain pills become secondary. You just keep those on hand when you run out of heroin. They will keep you well but they will not get you high.

OxyContin was coming into the picture. Everybody thought it was the perfect drug. They were showing these scientific ads on TV saying "Oh, this is the best drug on the planet for pain. It is not addictive. It's time released." And they looked like scientific case studies, where they would make it look businesslike and it didn't look like a commercial at all. Therein lies the problem. All these were commercials. All these companies that were making OxyContin were paying for these ads to look like scientific studies, to look like the drugs were not addictive. It was a facade and fake.

Well, millions of lives were destroyed by OxyContin. And if you keep up with the news, after decades they figured it out and got to the bottom of it. The companies that made OxyContin, the companies that screwed everyone's lives up and lied to the people, were made to pay billions of dollars back. They were found guilty of fraud and deceit. Many suicides, many addictions, and many deaths have been attributed to OxyContin. I became friends with a doctor's wife and almost had an affair with her. The doctor knew I was very close with his wife. I went to his Pain Clinic and he put me on two 60 mg. OxyContin a day. I made up a story and he believed me. I told him they were working great, but they were doing OK just keeping me well in between heroin.

So, in my other secret world, I was reaching a new comfort zone in the backstreets of Altoona, the hidden world where all the junkies and the junkyard dogs lie. They loved me. I had the $200,000 home. I had a Mercedes Benz. I had a Harley Davidson. I would come riding down in my motorcycle and these people clung to me. I was known as "the rich jewelry dude." In the afternoons, I actually became part of their gang and ran with them. Misery loves company, people. And it's where I felt safe. So sad to say. It was the beginning of my tragic end in jewelry and food after climbing to success and decades of hard work.

Everything was closing in on me. My father found a girlfriend in the VFW out in Cresson, PA, a very nice woman. She is now my stepmother. She slowly but surely moved into my Sylvan Hills house with my dad. I had my dad, Diane, Patty and Sue still helping me as well as Gilbert, paying him $400 just to ride with me to deliver food, help manage the jewelry stores, and make jewelry buys. He would help me with jewelry parties and shows and we'd party together. I was still seeing my children every other weekend. They were in another house. I was doing more and more heroin.

Once I got comfortable with shooting heroin, there was absolutely no maintaining. Throw that right out the window. I was dancing with the elites, all the doctors, doctors' wives, business people in Altoona, Clearfield, Oakland, Maryland, Lewistown, Harrisburg, and Pittsburgh. But I was also running with the junkyard dogs. And I was getting sicker and sicker and sicker and was up to about eight bags of heroin a day, still doing my two OxyContin. Oh, I was a man all right. My other hidden secret world was surfacing and I couldn't hide it. The junkies and junkyard dogs absolutely loved me. They would take turns using me. As long as I got my bags, whoever I was around got theirs. You see, in Altoona it was $40 per bag. At this time, New Jersey was coming into play. African Americans who came from the back streets of Jersey City found out they could come to Altoona and sell $6-$8 bags of heroin for $40 a pop. They were actually moving their families here, their mothers, their brothers, their sisters...coming to Altoona living in the backstreets where I was running during the day.

My businesses were starting to suffer. I had hundreds of thousands of dollars' worth of jewelry. Now the store in Tyrone was picking up but my girls Patty and Sue didn't like the drive from Duncansville to Tyrone. What they didn't realize is it was pulling all the people from all my areas-who would take a whole day and come to my jewelry store and spend massive amounts. You see, I did something different with the way I paid my girls. Not only did they make an hourly wage, but I gave them 8% commission on every sale. So if one of them sold $1,000 item, they made $80; if one of them sold $10,000 diamond, they made $800. And we were selling those. Patty would make special appointments with key people for big items. If I didn't have any stock, I'd just go to Precious Metals and Diamonds company and take it on consignment and bring it back. If a lady wanted a 3K diamond, I would go get four or five of them, let her choose which one she wanted and take the others back. What better system could you have? Precious Metals had millions and millions of dollars' worth of precious metals and jewelry. They were becoming one of the biggest distributors on the whole eastern coast. It was literally and figuratively a gold mine and the girls loved it. No one else was as good as I was as far as paying my help.

So I'm single. I'm falling in love with heroin every day needing more bags and spending more time in the backstreets of Altoona.

Patty came up to me one day and said, "Craig, this storefront opened up in Duncansville. I live a mile behind it. if you would move the jewelry store to Duncansville, I will be there all the time."

And Patty at the time was my main seller. She was responsible for big ticket item sales. I thought about it, talked it over with everybody and decided to make the move. It was only six months after I opened up in Tyrone. I blew everything up again-total chaos- moving these heavy damn jewelry cases and safes, getting out of my lease, and I opened up in Duncansville. I was still doing many jewelry shows and was getting known for them in Lewistown, Clearfield, and Oakland, Maryland. Everyone wanted to have a jewelry party. Everybody wanted food from me. I had a system put together that was working amazingly. It was just like every time I turned around, big ticket items were being ordered and sold - $600 here, $10,000 here, $500 here, whether it was food or filling a freezer up or selling a 10K tennis bracelet from the jewelry store or jewelry shows. Country clubs were calling me to do jewelry shows as I'm shooting heroin every day and befriending all these junkyard dogs and animals. I'm spending more and more time with them. I am high from the time I wake up until I go to sleep.

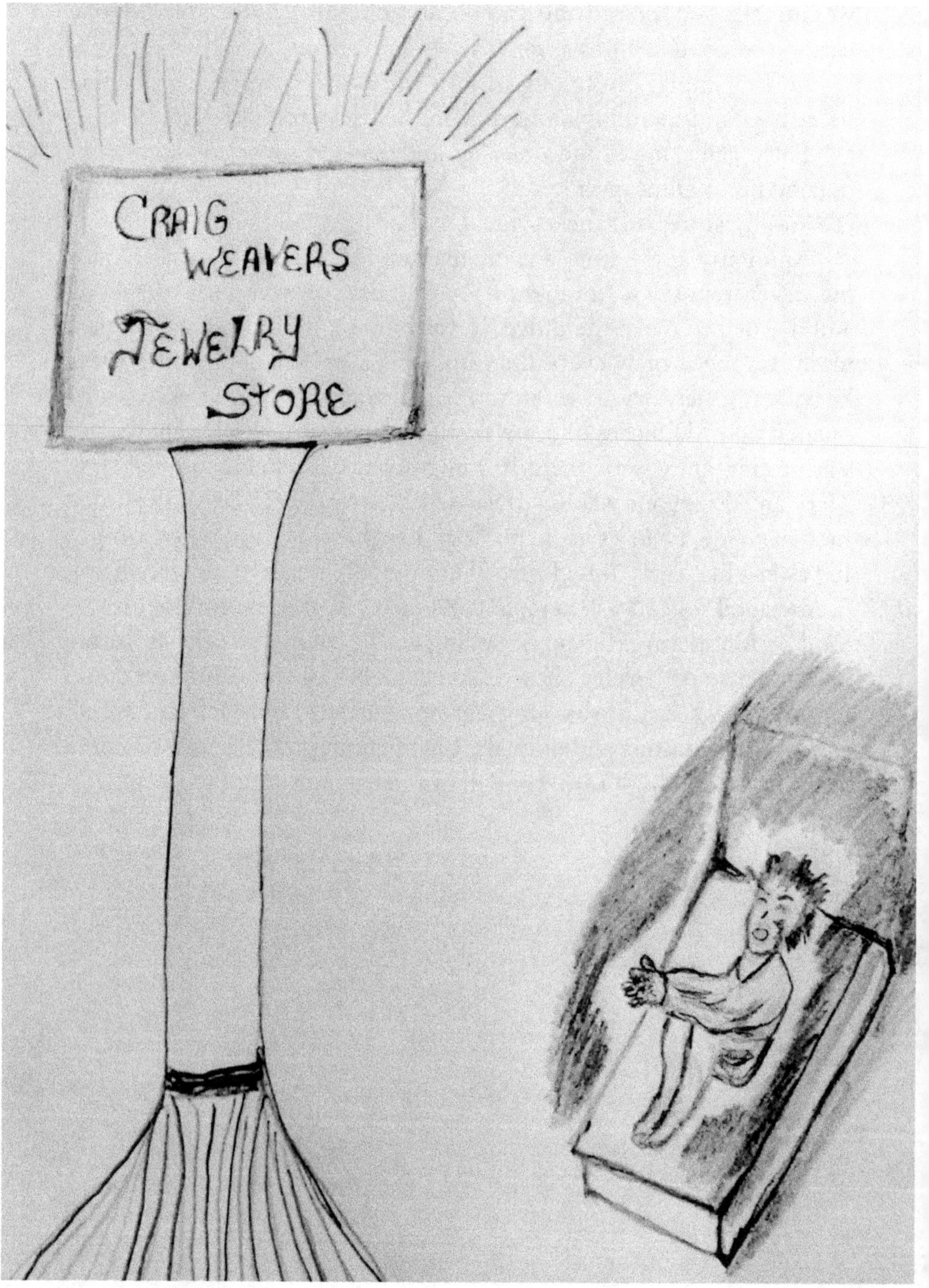
CRAIG
WEAVERS
JEWELRY
STORE

CHAPTER 9
NO MORE REALITY: I AM ANIMAL

Well, an incident happened in Duncansville. You see, Sue was there one day and I was in the office crushing up an OxyContin to snort it. If you snort them, they hit you ten times faster than if you eat them. They don't have to go through the digestive process. Well, Sue pokes her head in as I'm snorting a pill and runs to the doctor. Well, this doctor was a great customer of mine also, so was his wife. She loved me. She and I almost had a fling. I was too sick to have an affair. I wasn't in love with sex anymore. I wasn't in love with life anymore. I was in love with that needle going into my fucking arm and a minute later feeling those euphoric moments. That's all I cared about. Everything else was just to get through the day.

So this doctor was terrified when he found out I was snorting it. "Oh my God, he's an addict." Now instead of weaning me off of OxyContin, which can take a couple months- 120 mg a day-he got scared and shut me down that day.

Well, my stabilizing drug was no more. And heroin was hard to get sometimes in Altoona. It was a waiting game. It was a lying game.

"Oh, we're getting it tonight. They never made it back yet...we're getting it tomorrow." I was losing money.

I would give the junkies $500. "I got robbed. Got in some fights." Those were natural day occurrences with these people.

Both Sue and Patty were very leery of me. They knew. They knew I was addicted to opioids. I came clean with them but not as clean as I should've. I told them I had a problem. I never mentioned heroin. I just said it was about the pills.

So, I said to Patty and Sue, Diane and Dad, and Gilbert, "It's time for me to go get better."

Another rehab. But at this time in my life, ladies and gentlemen, things were moving so fast, things were building so quick, things were just going at such a fast pace every day with buying jewelry every other day and selling it and buying food and selling it, getting orders and delivering them to different cities. I couldn't take months off. I called the hospital in Johnstown, PA. They had a basement where they took in people that were addicted. It wasn't even a rehab. Basically, they threw you in the basement and didn't really know what they were doing. I just needed a place to hide. I was sick. I was weak and I was tired.

Patty and Sue stayed with me and I said, "Keep the store going. Keep the food going." And I left for Johnstown.

Now I'm in this basement curled up, 130 pounds, starting to go thru massive opioid withdrawal, sick, puking. Previously, I had ordered the biggest, nicest neon sign for my store. It was higher than every single sign in Altoona- "Craig Weaver's Jewelry Store"-a $15,000 sign! I was famous. But I'm in the hospital in Johnstown in a bed in the basement in the fetal position -puking, sweating. I don't want to think.

A nurse comes in. "Mr. Weaver, your manager from the store called, Patty. Your sign is being put up today." Oh my God, what a conundrum. Here they put up this gorgeous $15,000, thirty-foot sign you could see from everywhere -twenty miles around-in neon lights, flashing, "Craig Weaver's Jewelry Store." I had made it, folks. And here I am a sick and suffering heroin junkie in the fetal position in a cot in the basement of the Johnstown hospital. That memory is ingrained in my brain.

I was in there and a nurse comes walking in and I couldn't believe it...Nancy, my first childhood sweetheart in eighth grade, the first girl I ever kissed. We went thru eighth grade, ninth grade together, tenth grade. Then she moved and then I moved. But we were in whatever kind of love you can be in whenever you're twelve, thirteen, fourteen years old. And I thought about her a lot. Here she was- a nurse, my nurse.

"Craig," she said, "Oh my God!"

Well, I told her what happened. I told her all about me- the jewelry, the food. Here, she had just gotten divorced. She was single. She had a couple of beautiful daughters. Well, in amongst everything that was going on, my insanity showed. Didn't we hook up in the hospital. You see, one of the problems with withdrawal is your nerve endings are dead while you're using opioids. You can't have sex whenever you're a full-blown heroin addict. You can't get an erection; you can't get excited. You're just dead down there. But, about the third or fourth day of withdrawal, everything's waking up. You feel like you're sixteen years old again. You have a damn weapon. And it happened to hit exactly at the time when Nancy came in and was my nurse. And that's all we did.

Well, Nurse Nancy would be in my life now. You see, the seventh day Patty called me, Sue called me, Gilbert called me.

"We need you! Come out. Everything's going to shit. Get out of there!"

And Nancy talked me into it. "Craig, I'll come home with you. I will help you. We will make it thru this together."

Saturday morning, seven days in to my beginnings of withdrawal, I could hardly walk. You see, I wasn't just coming off opioids, I was coming off Xanax too. A doctor in Cresson had me on Xanax for seven years. They were the only thing that would put me to sleep at night. So I was actually withdrawing from barbiturates and opioids. We left the hospital, came home. Nancy stayed with me for a couple of weeks. It was me, dad, Nancy, and Diane living at home. I was so fucking sick. Nancy came with me, learned how to run the store, learned how to do the food. Well, hell, you couldn't blame her. She come walking in to ultra-successful businesses with multi successful snowballing patterns at the same time. Everything was growing and she saw this. She was a very smart person. She clung by me and learned everything and met everybody. Patty and Sue and everyone was kind of behind me and very supportive at first. That would not last.

I did an advertisement where for an hour a radio station comes over- Forever Broadcasting- where they do a show with you and you talk on the radio. This was my first clue that things were getting ready to break up. Patty's there, Sue's there. It cost me $2,000. Even though I'm sick, I'm on the radio telling people to get the hell over to the Duncansville store. I introduce Patty in front of thousands of people. She would not get on the microphone. She stood back there and kept shaking her head, "No." I was so embarrassed, ladies and gentlemen. She wasn't with me.

She and Sue did a jewelry show at the Sylvan Hills Country Club in Hollidaysburg and I wasn't allowed to go and I'm the owner. They were too embarrassed to let me do it. In four hours, at this jewelry show, they sold $11,000 worth of jewelry. And the owner of Kranich's Jewelry, a member of the Sylvan Hills Country Club, was also there.

He kept shaking his head saying, "This guy is going to make it big."

He watched everything and said I had a beautiful display. Patty and Sue come back to my house and I gave them their commission.

OK now, Nurse Nancy moves in. Patty and Sue leave me. They were too embarrassed- "Craig Weaver is nothing but a drug addict."

And they used to look up to me.

In fact, when I first brought Nancy home, Patty told Nancy when they met, "You are with a giant of a man. If you're going to help him, you have some big shoes to fill." I'll never forget that. That made me feel good.

But no, no, I wasn't a giant of a man. I wasn't a man. In my mind, I was a drug addict. In my mind-deep, deep back in my mind's eye, I was nothing, I was nobody, I didn't deserve this. I am a low life heroin junkie. But yet I'm dancing with the elites. I'm selling them tons of items and they all respect me. This is the epitome of two lives in one, ladies and gentlemen. This is what addicts have to go through.

This is why I am reaching out and letting everyone know how insidious this disease is. I wasn't a bad son of a bitch trying to get good. I was a sick bastard suffering, caught up in this evil disease, that was killing me. And I didn't know where to turn, didn't know who to go to. I needed months to get better. I could not take months. I was caught in a living hell. Hell on earth is and always will be the best name for what I went through-hell on earth inside my head.

Here I sit now, broke, sixty-two years old, but I'll be honest with you. I am happy just to wake up and be able to lift my head off that fucking pillow. I am happy just to not feel that pain that is inside your broken brain when you are addicted and withdrawal is hitting you like it does every morning when you open your eyes. It is so good just to be clean. Please, if you are addicted to something, if you can't get off something, there is life after addiction. It takes time, if you're on a lot, if you've been addicted for years. Trust me, just get it in your head-two months-sixty days. No matter where you go, what happens, if you can keep those drugs out of your system for sixty days, you will find a new kind of high. It's called life, a new kind of freedom. I can smell a rose now and enjoy the fragrance. Life is good. Money isn't everything.

So Nancy was running the store, Diane was running the store. Dad would go and pick up some jewelry. I was just trying to maintain day after day. I'd sneak down to those damn back alleys to be with these people just trading and swapping and stealing drugs-buying heroin for $40 a bag, becoming friends with the Jersey boys. I started staying at Nancy's house past Ebensburg, Pennsylvania. She had her own house too, with her daughters. Then we'd come back home. It was winter and the weather was bad. Nancy started stealing Percocet from the hospital to give to me because it was only a few months after I left the Johnstown hospital and with the barbiturates and the opioids the withdrawal was unbearable. She would come home with Percocet after work every day from the hospital. So therefore, I started taking the damn things. I made it awhile but I was too sick to get well. And I jumped into the stress; I jumped into my world again.

Well, here behind the scenes, Nurse Nancy was moving in quicker than I even knew. She actually was going to the school district in Hollidaysburg and got her kids set up to start school there. She was getting ready to move her whole family to my house in Sylvan Hills without me knowing it. So I'm struggling one day, back on heroin. That didn't last long.

And I said to her, "Nancy, I'm dying again. I can't do this. I'm back to using. I'm falling apart. I should've never left the Johnstown Hospital after seven days."

Well, here comes White Deer Run.

Nancy took over the jewelry store with Diane and dad. She even made some food deliveries.

White Deer Run introduced me to methadone which will be very key later on in life. I'm about forty-five and I find myself in a very good rehab. I'll never forget the first day there when I was staying in a little room about 200 yards from the meeting room of the building. It was the first morning I woke up there and I had to meet everyone in the meeting room. And I looked over and saw my socks, my underwear, my clothes lying on a chair.

I looked at those clothes and I thought to myself, "I can't do this, I'll never do this."

And I wasn't meaning going to the meeting. I could not put a pair of socks on and my underwear. I was so sick and weak. That was one of the hardest mornings of my life. Well, that afternoon they gave me 30 mg. of methadone. Son of a bitch, two hours later, I felt so good- not high, not up there in the clouds. I felt normal. I felt well. I felt like I was never on drugs in my life. It was a miracle.

People! You're probably wondering why I never stayed clean after all the times I ran out, my rehab tries, jail, etc. Let's get the truth. Once you become acutely addicted, after a couple of years, the make-up of your brain changes. The brain rewires itself. Subconsciously you desire the unique opioid high but it's chemically induced so it's different- unnatural. You actually do not feel OK or even just plain good for many many months. It's hard to live knowing you just aren't like you used to be. TIME is key. You must go months and months without any form of mind-altering substance. It's hard, so tough knowing that a couple pills will give you a break. Every addict, please hear me! Tough it out. Stay busy. Plan your day. Just know that one day you will awaken and everything will be lifted, all the tension and stress, all the pain and anxiety will be GONE! Maybe four, five, or six months but you will be freed from hell on earth. Do not let doctors fill your head with anti-depressants or mood elevators, only for a short while if you must. But get off everything and LIVE.

OK, a brief summary, things were moving quick. Now, let's review, I caught Doll screwing around with her old boyfriend Tom. So she moved back to Juniata at her place. And Dad and I were living in my place. My addiction caught up with me. I went to a supposed rehab in the basement of Johnstown hospital. It wasn't a rehab; they knew not what they were doing. I met my high school sweetheart. I came crawling out of there seven days later. At that time, my $15,000 sign, the highest sign in all of Altoona, Duncansville, and Holidaysburg was put up. And I'm lying in a fetal position in the basement of a freakin' hospital suffering, sick, addicted. You talk about a conundrum. This was one of the lowest points of my life. Everybody was rooting for me to become successful. My status was moving up. Doctors were coming to my house just to hang out. They weren't my people though.

I'm a middle-class type of guy, a hard worker. I don't let money change me. In fact, that's part of the problem. I didn't care about money as much as I should have. I was playing with tons of money but never thought of my future. I just lived for that day. Now that I was way way sick in my addiction, too sick to even go out and get my opioids. I go to a dungeon and I bring Nancy home. Dad's with Diane, his love, his true love. Nancy and I are going back and forth from her house outside of Ebensburg to mine. Of course, Diane and Nancy didn't get along too well, a little bit of turmoil there. You talk about insanity. I bring a girl home to live with me, going thru massive withdrawal in a hospital, while my life is crumbling. Then I'm falling in love. I didn't know how to love. Nancy, who was a nurse, could give two shits about addiction and she started feeding me Percocet she stole from the hospital. I got sick again probably a month and a half later. Patty and Sue, my two part time managers, were really falling back and were losing all faith and hope in me but Diane was still with me.

Before I went to White Deer Run, I met with Nancy and we went over everything. I gave her addresses of food deliveries and I told her what I needed her to do in the jewelry store. And to give her credit, she did a hell of a job while I was away.

Now in White Deer Run, I was introduced to methadone 30 mg. I never felt better. I thought I was cured. Well methadone is stronger than heroin. You see, what it does is it still affects you but it doesn't throw your endorphins into high gear. You get every other benefit which is pain control, no withdrawal but you don't get high; you don't get near as high. Methadone is becoming very popular as a maintenance program. We'll be talking more about that. It's a double-edged sword. There's a lot of bad with methadone but there is a lot of good with methadone. As I'm speaking to you now, I am still on 28mg a day, which is a very low amount. I'm working my way to zero. I've been on it for twelve years. The problem with methadone is the withdrawal is as intense if not more and lasts longer than heroin. So you must be weaned off of it so slow, maybe 1 or 2mg. every other week because you actually feel even a small amount taken away.

Now in White Deer Run, I was so sick I didn't know how to get dressed that first morning. But after the methadone I was fine. I went to classes. I was being a good boy. I was learning. But what I didn't realize is they wean you off of methadone within four or five days. They get you kicking, they get you motivated and you start going back out into the community there. But within four or five days when you hit zero, you are back to full withdrawal. But you see you're already in the community, you're already part of the whole rehab. I can remember just suffering through. I had to walk one foot after the other.

Then the phone calls started. "We need you out. The store isn't running well. The steak and seafood business is going haywire."

So after twelve days, I left. That is the problem. Do I on one hand, stay in there for a couple months and lose everything I worked for-for years and years and years? It would fall. It would not survive. Bills, the businesses, my family, my responsibilities- I would walk out of that rehab probably $50,000 in debt with people pissed off at me, losing customers. I mean, what do you do? That's why addiction is hell on earth.

So, after twelve days, I came back and I tried to make it again. It wasn't long enough. I didn't know what Nancy was doing, but in that condition, I couldn't think right and I was still semi-insane. She started her Percocet thing again. So, behind my back, Nancy goes to Hollidaysburg and signs her two daughters up for high school. I think they were in eleventh or twelfth grade. She has her house up for sale which I didn't know. And she had it in her head that she was moving in Sylvan Hills with her family. Now that's with Diane and Dad still there.

No, it wasn't happening.

So, one day in the jewelry store, her and her mom were visiting.

I said, "Nancy, we're done."

Her mom looked at me and said, "What?"

I said, "We're done." I said, "We're over."

They were flabbergasted. You see, once again in the back of my mind, in my mind's eye, I knew this wasn't going to work from the get go. How in the hell could I take on another family- two daughters in high school, moving them into my house with dad and Diane? And I wasn't even in love with her. It could've evolved into love if I would've been straight and we would've seen each other for around a year. She was a good girl. But I knew what she was after, moving everything so quickly, doing things behind the scenes without telling me. You don't think she saw dollar signs-with hundreds of thousands of dollars' worth of diamonds, gold, and precious metals and finding out how much I made selling food!!

I remember the day I did that. I was sick. I felt like crap. I think I was doing around five to six bags of heroin a day, but heroin was hit or miss in Altoona. You see, it was coming in from Jersey City like I said.

And these guys were so unreliable. They'd say, "I'll be back in a day," and wouldn't come back for a week. Or if you "front" them some money, you don't see them until you track them down. They're all packing; that is, they all carry guns and knives. These are all inner-city boys from the "hood." As you will find out later, I'll be visiting the "hood." Buckle up for that one. I have scars to prove it.

So I kicked Nancy's ass back to Ebensburg. My ears were still burning a day after her mom and her left. I'm sick. Patty leaves me. Sue leaves me. Diane's hanging on trying to maintain my business for me. I do give her credit. Dad's wife now was very good to me back in those days.

I was becoming allies with part of the gang of junkyard dogs. There was a black guy, "Taz", who had one wooden leg, and was in his sixties. Well, he was the main man on the back streets of Altoona- 6th Avenue. His whole household was addicted to opioids; the whole street was addicted to opioids. We called it "Heroin Alley." Oh, I was meeting everybody back there- junkies and sick people. It was another world, ladies and gentlemen, a secret, sick, disgusting world right in the middle of a town. These people were animals and I was slowly transforming into that myself. I can remember spending hours down there in the afternoons.

Now I would only go out and sell food when I needed money. Customers were starting to get pissed off and were seeing me physically look bad. I was starting to miss deliveries, miss appointments, get there late, get there early, not bring the right product. And of course, my cleanliness was affected. I had a warehouse in Sylvan Hills and I packed a lot of food. Cleanliness is key. When you're a heroin addict, there's no way, but I was cleaner than most. I had a good constitution, thank God. At first, even during my heroin addiction, I wasn't stealing and ripping people off yet. Oh, I was starting to lie. In fact, I was lying a lot - making excuses where I was at, where I was going, disappearing for days. Diane kept the store going. I started just going to my best customers. I dropped Harrisburg and Pittsburgh. You see, what saved me, for a long time, was most of my areas were out of town. So those people couldn't see me or hear about me becoming a drug addict. I could keep it from them for a long time.

So I started hanging with "Taz". His wife couldn't stand anybody. He was black. She was white. She was an addict and she stayed in her own space in this dark gloomy three story home. She was always in the living room with a little TV- and black curtains, a brown rug, and walls painted dark green. That room was like a cave or animal's lair and daylight or bright light was shunned.

Well, "Taz" had a third floor. He called it "The Jungle." That's where we went. There were about six, eight, ten of us hard core heroin junkies. I was "The Jewelry Dude" with money. I even started taking my jewelry displays. I always carried extra in my truck to go to these guy's row houses to buy heroin and started trading them jewelry for bags of dope. Hell, the bags only cost them $6, $7 a bag. They were $40 a bag in Altoona. So, yeah, they started calling me and saying, "Hey, I got some shit. Bring your jewelry, "Jewelry Dude."

I'll never forget, I took one couple to my house in Sylvan Hills. They were both "gone" living down there in "Little Philly" as I called it. Dad and Diane had moved out. They decided they wanted their own house. I think Dad knew what was going on. Diane still hung in there with the jewelry store.

So I was alone living in this beautiful home. By now, it was listed at $200,000. I lived there for about nine years and only owed about $55,000 on it. But I was all alone there. So I started becoming buddies with these people- "Taz" and the others. Anyways I took these two people to my house and they could not believe it. Boyfriend and girlfriend, they had a twelve-year-old son. Their apartment had three feet thick garbage on the floors-kitchen and living room. The boy was out of control. I sat in their house for hours many days. It's what you did. You always had to wait on drugs. You took your money and you waited until they left and until they came back. "Oh, I'll be back in forty minutes, three hours, four hours, five hours."

So I finally brought these two junkies to my house. Big mistake. The next thing, the whole gang of them, knew I was for real and couldn't believe it. Oh, I became very popular. So we had a gang and started going to "Taz's" house to shoot dope on his third floor. I ended up buying most of the time. I started doing crack cocaine then because all these guys from Jersey City would bring back heroin and crack. Every time I'd order bags of heroin, now I was ordering bags of crack- $40 a bag of heroin and $20 a rock for crack. This was beginning to be my world. My other world, the life that I had built over two and a half decades was becoming further and further away. It was getting uncomfortable to enter that world. The sicker I got, the more addicted I got- the more I stayed with my miserable junkie friends. The next thing I was up to ten bags a day, twelve bags a day. Now this life I was living was getting dangerous. Hell, I had a gun pulled on me by one of the Jersey City boys because I was nice to his damn girlfriend. He brought her back with him at an apartment and he wasn't home one day. He was supposed to have a few bags for me and I thanked her and called her "honey."- "Thank you, honey."

Next thing I know- I'm at Taz's house; my truck's out back and he saw it. He flies up the third floor and has a gun pointed right between my freakin' eyes. He had the gun on me and literally made me go back and apologize to his wife. And I did it. I was going thru withdrawal and wasn't the man I used to be. And I had a fucking gun pointed and he would shoot me. These guys from Jersey City killed people. They told me stories. You see, the street they lived on was River Street. This huge river about half a mile wide flowed right across the road. And then these row houses where they all lived were crack houses, heroin houses. And they'd kill people and throw them in the damn river. No one ever reported it; no one ever called the police. These guys were the real deal. They were all junkies themselves but they learned how to handle heroin better than me...for a while. Nobody can handle heroin forever or for a long, long time. You just can't. The only one I ever heard that did heroin and stayed successful was Ray Charles, the black singer who was blind. I read all about this man. He did heroin all his life- a couple bags a day. How the hell he did that, to this day, I have no idea. But he's the only one I know of. In my own decades of drug use, I found you cannot, repeat- CANNOT maintain with heroin.

Diane and I were still doing some jewelry shows at the Heidelberg club in Sylvan Hills with a few of my customers. But I was becoming so sick I couldn't do much of anything except shoot heroin. I finally left the jewelry store. I was two months behind in rent. I packed all my jewelry- 2,800 bracelets, 3,200 rings, 3,600 gold chains-just an amazing amount of jewelry. It was $800,000 worth, my cost. And I owned it! I owed nothing on it. My God, how long that took to get. It took eight jewelry cases, these big handbags, to carry it all. Each jewelry case held anywhere from $50,000 to $200,000 worth. And I'm carrying them around in my damn truck like it was nothing. Insanity!

It hits me so hard now, seeing what I had. And the worst thing about it, ladies and gentlemen, is I worked for every penny. I was a go-getter. I had a work ethic like no other; I would work fifteen, eighteen, nineteen hours a day making food deliveries. And I'm losing everything. Now, I have $800,000 in jewelry and all these food customers, a house that I only owe $55,000 on. But I am insane and sick and getting worse and worse. My immunity was going up and up and up and I needed more and more. When you have a ton of money and access to heroin and you're an addict, that equation leads to death! I had so many customers waiting and wondering where I was. A lot of them figured me out. Rumors were spreading around. It was getting worse and worse. I tried another rehab that year. I was about forty-seven. I went to Cove Forge but the sixth day I had to leave. I couldn't do it. I had too much money out there. I had too much jewelry. I could sell a damn ring so easy. Oh, I could get up money so easily with having $800,000 worth of jewelry. My liquid cash was low but I hustled. But I was falling behind on my $1,200 a month mortgage but I owned everything else.

So after the six days of the rehab and coming back, I ran into Doll. Here she was with some guy that beat the shit out of her and broke her arm. She had a cast on. We started dating again. Now this gets totally absurd. Doll was addicted to crack. Crack is mostly a mental addiction. You only feel like shit for a day or two after you quit using it. But that mental craving, that mental addiction with crack makes your endorphins dance so crazy and so wild for about three to five minutes when you inhale it. But then you lose it after five minutes. You lose your buzz and go down below normal. As high as you went, you go that much lower. And you want more so bad, so quick. Once people touch a crack pipe, they don't let go. My sister sadly was one of those people.

So we were a great team at this stage of our lives. Somehow, she had kept her job as a medical secretary. She was in Juniata and I was at my house. Dad and Diane were at a nice residential area about three miles away from me. I started staying at Doll's a lot. In fact, I'd stay there for three or four days at a time. My house was just too big. I had my food over there. I was getting up enough strength to sell maybe a day or two a week. But it was getting harder and harder. I wasn't keeping up with anything. My bills were piling up. I wasn't seeing my kids.

The last time I saw my kids, I'll never forget this. I had them over for a weekend and was on heroin. I ran out when they were there. I couldn't leave them there alone. I packed them up in my truck, rode to "Little Philly," parked the truck in the back alley where Taz lived, and went up to the third floor. I let my kids sit in that truck for two hours just for me to get some damn heroin. That was the last time I picked my kids up. When I came back to reality a little bit later that day, I just shook my head. I said, "No more, no more. I am not fit to have the responsibility of being with my kids. I was not going to take them down with me." They were very functional kids.

So it was me and Doll and all the junkies in "Little Philly." And we were becoming friends with the Jersey City boys because they brought crack home too. I was buying enough crack and enough heroin for both of our habits. I started doing crack too, with the heroin; it's called a "speedball." I almost blew my heart out a few times. Life was changing for me. I was losing control. I was wearing the same clothes for days. I wasn't washing; my hygiene was terrible.

All Doll and I were were drug buddies. There was no relationship there. We were just living off each other. I guess years later I found out she was having a heyday with my eight jewelry cases because I had no idea what my inventory was. I couldn't keep track of it. And I found out she would grab a bunch of jewelry and take it into this Altoona tattoo shop and just move it out from there. She was having fun. And you know what, "Good for her." I mean when you're an insane addicted animal, you have no morals, you have no compass; you have no direction. You will lie, cheat, and steal. I probably would've done it myself if the situation would've been reversed at that time. I can't blame her.

The reality was I lost "Me." I lost Craig. That outgoing, intelligent, friendly, life loving guy was gone. I remember I used to set the alarm at her house. She still had to go to work and be there by I think six. But I'd set the alarm before she got up. It was four in the morning. You know why? - It was to get up and shoot a bag of heroin. And I was so numb in the morning and so out of whack, I couldn't focus my eyes so I couldn't find a vein. I would miss and have these sores on my arms and feet. When you miss, you can get a nasty sore, a bump, and it stays there for days. So, yeah, I was setting the alarm for 4 o'clock every morning, going to the kitchen table and shooting a bag of dope. That's how I started my damn day.

So now it's Doll and me and my jewelry and all we're doing is making sure we have enough heroin and crack for both of us. When I started living with Doll again, we were both going down, down, down. I was basically only selling jewelry to the black dudes giving me heroin. Doll would come with me selling food and we'd make 6, 7, $800 and we'd use most of that money for heroin and crack cocaine.

The good world, the world I left, was afraid of me by now. All my friends, associates, business people pretty well didn't even know where I went. I disappeared from them. I was only seeing outlying customers -the further away from Altoona, the better. Rumors were spreading rapidly. I missed my employees so much. I had it made with Patty, Sue, Diane, my dad's wife.

One day I got a phone number from one of the guys in "Little Philly" of a dude in Pittsburgh who gave pretty good buys on cocaine and crack. I called him and he talked me into coming. So Doll and I take off to Clearfield, Philipsburg to sell food and ended up in Pittsburgh that evening. This guy lived in a row house, had a thirteen-foot boa python and he'd let it roam around the damn room. I remember shitting myself the first time I saw that thing. Holy hell, it crawled over us and phew, I thought for sure I was going to be eaten by that son of a bitch. But I didn't care. It was $20 a bag of heroin, $20 for a nice crack rock. I'd buy 6, 7, $800 worth. We'd drive home, go into her bedroom, turn the phones off, lock the house up and we'd be in there for about a day and a half. Doll started shooting me up. I was becoming an animal. I kept us both going in heroin and crack.

OK, now remember the life I had built before, a guy who had thousands of customers, who had built up an empire. Even though I was an opioid addict, I still maintained. I was good to people. I kept a good appearance. I was doing everything pretty damn right. I'm going to show you now where heroin will take you. This is heading straight down to hell on earth. OK, I'm doing crack and heroin. Dad and Diane knew I was sick and what I was doing. I'd spend a day or two over at their house when I couldn't walk or talk anymore. I was starting to have trouble selling enough of anything to get cash. And then when I'd sell something on the phone, I'd go back to Doll's and we'd get some heroin and crack. I was only making one food trip a week being so sick. I get sick writing about this. I must lie down.

One night before a food trip, staying overnight at my father's house, I saw a jar of pennies. I was broke. The only money I had was in food but I wasn't going to be selling it for another day or two. And I needed a bag of heroin. I ran out. No matter how hard I tried, I could never keep heroin for the next day. The more I had, the more I did. So I'm totally out. It's about 7 o'clock, 8 o'clock at night. I'm actually trying to go through withdrawal. I'm over at my dad's house trying to get better. It's one of those times, when in your brain you think you can conquer this and go through withdrawal without being in a rehab. Bullshit! Especially heroin withdrawals, they are intense. So I break this jar open and I'm counting pennies and couldn't get up enough. So I had been going to this restaurant in Altoona when I was running out of money and talked them into cashing checks for me. I did this maybe two times. They heard about me. They were at my store. The restaurant owner did not know how bad I was or if I was even on drugs at all. I could still put on a good act. So this particular night I'm going to take a check and go to this restaurant and get it cashed. I couldn't get up enough for heroin, not with pennies-$40 a bag with Taz. I didn't have the money to go to Pittsburgh. You always have days like this where you just can't find anything.

So I get in the truck, my seafood truck. I take off down 6th Avenue in Altoona. And I am so out of it. I hit a car on the right of me, a parked car, as I'm traveling about forty miles an hour. I smacked into it, veered off of it and kept on going. Well, the lady behind me got her cell phone out, called the cops. She witnessed it. Next thing I knew there's about three or four police cars behind me, sirens blaring, lights glaring. I happen to go out on 17th street in Altoona, the main drag- a four lane highway and pulled in the middle of it. The cops were right behind me and stopped. I got out. They told me to get back in. Now, all of a sudden, there's six police cars, pretty well surrounding me. Now remember I'm going to this restaurant to write a bad check, get some cash, and go to my old buddy Taz's to get a bag of heroin. Well, the cops looked at me and saw that I was disheveled and my eyes were glassy.

"Would you step out of the car, sir. We're going to give you a test."

Well, first I did the breathalyzer and passed it. They wanted to give me another test. I actually passed it too-counting backwards and walking a straight line. And there are six patrol cars and the funny thing not the funny thing but the crazy thing is that my truck was full of needles all over the floor. It was filthy. There was drug paraphernalia, old bags of empty heroin. And they never saw one needle. They were everywhere. Then they checked if I had insurance. My insurance lapsed. So the cop writes me up for "hit and run," no insurance.

But because he heard of me, he knew me, I gave him some lame excuse like "I just got new medication that really "zapped" me out." He believed me. This is the owner of Craig Weaver's Jewelry stores.

"We can't let you drive this vehicle. You're going to have to call someone to get you."

Now here comes insanity. I'm not worried one bit about the tickets I was getting or the trouble I was in, having no insurance. You know what I was worried about? I need that bag of heroin. I need that bag of dope.

So I looked up at the cop. I'll never forget this.

I said, "OK, can you call me a tow truck? I can take my truck right out here to a restaurant and I'm friends with the owner and leave it there for the night."

Now, here's the kicker. I had no cash. Remember I was going to the restaurant to write a bad check to get cash to buy heroin. OK, I had no cash but I did have a credit card that was no good. It had nothing on it. The cop calls the tow truck. The tow truck comes. It's 7 o'clock in the evening.

I said, "All I have is this credit card but I'm local. Why don't I just give it to you tonight after you tow me. It's only about four blocks down the road-to the restaurant. And you can have my credit card and I'll come pick it up tomorrow." I knew the credit card had no money on it but I didn't give a shit.

I was an animal that needed my heroin for my endorphins to function. Therefore, I would go to any depths to get it- lie, cheat, steal. I was no longer a human being; I was a fucking animal. So I'm sitting in with the tow truck driver bullshitting with him. We get to the restaurant. Cops are gone. He leaves me go, pulls in. I get out of the tow truck, go in the restaurant, and talk the owner into cashing another check. I have no clue why he was doing that. It was my reputation, I guess. It was for $200. I kept them low. You see, I had done it before to him but I guess it didn't clear his bank, my bank and get back to him yet. This was before everything got automated and fast. So I did it again.

I ended up at Taz's house with $200, sitting up in his third-floor shooting heroin- I got about five or six bags.

Now that's just one story there about one evening -with no heroin, no money. Somehow, I made it back out for another day of selling food with Doll. Clearfield was my best area where I could always sell. I probably had over 100 customers just in Clearfield, Pennsylvania alone. All the employees of the banks, homeowners, business people-everyone there bought off of me. Nice town, very close people-everyone knows everybody and they all get along. I love Clearfield. I almost moved there. So Doll and I are in Clearfield, then we're in Pittsburgh, then back to her house in her bedroom for a day and a half. Now don't get me wrong. Doll was good looking and she was hot! And you'd think in her bedroom for a day and a half with heroin and crack cocaine, we would have one hell of a night also. No, nope. Sex was gone.

Oh, I think back when we first met, my wife and I weren't getting along. We weren't having sex. I think we went two years without having sex. The only reason we had a second child was because I went to Alaska with my father and two uncles. It was one of the times when I came out of a rehab. I wasn't bad yet. We spent fourteen days on the Kenai peninsula fishing for salmon and driving around. I was with our guide when he shot a big bull moose. I remember catching salmon 60 inches long, 50 inches long, going back to a cabin, throwing them right on a grill. My uncles are great guys. But I didn't have enough medication with me and spent half the trip sick. I can remember standing in the middle of Silver Creek as they called it. It came right off the ocean into a stream and the salmon were running everywhere. You were in about three feet of water and you could see these runs of salmon like herds. I remember they were coming to my right and to my left; I'd see them go in between my legs. Some of them looked as big as me. And I'm standing there in this gorgeous wooded area on the Kenai peninsula in fucking Alaska and I'm sick. I'm not enjoying it. I had a headache. I was stressed. I was sick in my stomach. I dealt with that...I went back and forth from being sick, to being OK and then I'd take whatever pills I had left. I was trying to ration them. And I had the "crappy" pills, Darvocet, Tylenol #3s. It was so hard to keep the good shit flowing all the time. And you always ended up, as we used to call it, with "junk pills". So I'm in Alaska with "junk pills". But when we come home after two weeks, I was cleaned out enough from not having the real strong medication flowing through my veins and killing my body, that I had sex with my wife Kim. We were still married at the time. And that one night, after about a year and a half with no sex -before I met Doll, we had Kelsey. One time.

So there were Lisle and Kelsey. It's very hard to talk about. I really screwed up. As of now, I'm sitting here with no relationship with my children. I tried to get them back about four or five years ago and they didn't want a thing to do with me. Even after nine years clean, they are under the assumption that Daddy is terrible, bad, disgusting. And the only thing I was doing was staying away from them while I was so dysfunctional, not myself, an animal, not able to care for them. I stayed away from them because I knew that if I would've been in their lives back then, they would've formed some type of dysfunctionality. It would've screwed them up in some way for them to be around me when I was going through that stuff. I knew that because I went through it with my father. I couldn't stand being with him at times. And I didn't want them to see me like that. And it hurts so bad. I miss them so much. And my ex-wife is bitter. She loved me and she just thinks I left her for Doll. She has no clue how sick I was, no clue how addicted I was. No clue about addiction whatsoever. Basically, she thinks all that happened was not due to drugs. But add the drug addiction to all that and then you have one terrible father.

The saddest thing I want everyone to know- if you meet me, you will know or would know- I have the biggest heart, the most love of anybody. I'm a giver. I'm a great person. And I could have the best relationship with my kids. We could be having so much fun. Our personalities are so outgoing, so positive, so intelligent, and so filled with laughter. I know I would mesh beautifully with Kelsey and Lisle again as back years ago. We used to have a lot of good times. I took Lisle to a concert. I took him fishing. Kelsey and I would spend nights where it was just "Me and Her Night," as we called it. We'd go and load up with goodies at the grocery store and come home and just watch TV together, just feeding our faces and laughing. What I'm hoping, what I pray for, is my kids read this book. I want them to really read it.

Lisle and Kelsey, read it. Feel me. Maybe by some leap of faith, if you two read this book, and know what really happened to me, we can get back together again. I will get back together with you guys. A lot of time is wasting. I am getting older. I would love to spend the rest of my days with a great relationship because I love you. I always will and I always did. So if you do read this book, please come and see me. Give me a call.

So Doll and I were shells. She was as addicted to cocaine as I was to heroin. There was no sex. The point I was going to make was I can remember back to the day when she first started helping me. When we met, it was some of the most exciting times in my life. We waited for months to have sex. We literally grew to love each other. The more we were together, the more we couldn't be apart. And did we have so much fun. Life was so exciting. We would make plans and carry them out. We were in love. She wasn't in love with Tom, the state cop that was just taking care of her. And Kim and I weren't in love anymore. In fact, Kim had a crush on one of my best friends who she's married to right now.

And look at us now...driving to Pittsburgh, never even talking, getting loaded at this dealer's crack house, driving home and just doing all the drugs we bought. We spent all our time locked up in a bedroom, trying to get higher and higher but you can't. You just have to keep doing it so you don't get sick. Your endorphins don't know what the hell's going on. They're 10,000 times higher than they're supposed to be and after a while you just become numb; you don't even feel it. You are not high only cold stoned zombified!

The next time I was broke, Doll was at work. I had about six bags of jewelry left. I was starting to get robbed and didn't give two shits about it. Doll was stealing it. I was broke this day and I needed a bag of heroin so bad. It was about 10 in the morning and raining out. I take off to Sheetz and there's a Special Olympics jar on the counter filled with dollar bills and change. I grab the son of a bitch off the counter and went out to my truck and left. I pulled over and counted the money. This one only had $13. I went to the second Sheetz store in Altoona, grabbed the Special Olympics jar, walked out, in front of everybody. It was about noon now and I'm sitting in the parking lot ready to pull out.

Out comes the manager. "Hey mister, people saw you take the Special Olympics container."

I looked at him and I said, "Yeah, I saw a guy. He ran right by me with it."

He looked in my truck and the jar was right beside me. I handed him the jar. He went back into the Sheetz store. I pulled out and left.

I went to a third Sheetz store, walked in, grabbed the damn third Special Olympics jug off the counter.

Yes, it was me, Craig Weaver, Craig Weaver Jewelry, "The Meat Man," the businessman, the success, the American dream, the hard worker... Now I'm an animal, maybe even lower, subconsciously praying I get caught and thrown in jail or get killed or something terrible happens to me, so I can quit living in this "hell on earth," suffering constantly.

But I took that third jar and there was a lot in that one-about $40. I ride to Taz's house and walk up to the third floor. He had heroin but you couldn't get a bag unless you gave him $40. I threw that money out on the floor and I remember the look he gave me seeing the Special Olympics jugs. He thought I was nuts and he was as nuts as I was. And I got my bag of heroin. Just another day in the life of a heroin junkie. So many out there need saved.

Now all this is taking place pretty quick. I was addicted to pills for a couple decades, actually three and a half. I had a few good years where I was clean for a minute, but I always relapsed. But now that I'm on heroin, it's just a fast road down. So things are moving kind of fast but slow for me as I was caught in time -in a place-in HELL ON EARTH. I'm saying it again. That's where I was, ladies and gentlemen. Those three words say so much. After going through decades of opioid addiction. I don't know how I'm still here. I don't know how I'm still healthy. Hell, my liver even regenerated. I'm not really healthy but I work out every day and bust my butt. I have gotten my body back in the best shape it's going to be and I'm going to keep her as long as I can. Although I have pains everywhere, I ache and have sciatica, I'm working three jobs right now.

But back then, it's like you're caught in this small, small world. Everything is evil. Everything is negative. Everything is down. There is no living. You are dead but alive. You have no soul. You have no love to give. The only thing you're in love with is that fucking drug. And I mean every word of that. I was in love with of the art of shoving that needle somewhere in my body and finding that vein and as soon as that blood comes up you know you hit paydirt, because it was so hard to find anymore. Most of my veins were collapsing. I think I was around this time up to twenty bags a day. Once you get the blood to rise up in that needle and you know you're three to four seconds away from that rush, you are in love with that.

And I'm hanging with all the people that do nothing but shoot heroin in their bodies. That's all you can do. You have to. You have to keep that shit in you or you won't be walking, you won't be talking, you won't be functioning. You will be in a fetal position "puking" your guts out. To know that can happen to you within a day's time is the scariest thing on the planet. It feels like you're standing at the edge of this huge cliff looking down a couple thousand feet to rocks. And you're standing there every morning. That's how scared you are, living every day of your life like that. And don't ever get this wrong, addicts are very intelligent people. Imagine waking up every morning broke, with no money, but you have a $300 habit, some $500 a day to just function, to just walk amongst people, to live on this planet. Mine was getting up to $600 a day. Every day of my life I had to have that or I would be sick. It's called "below well" in the drug world. You end up living most of your life "below well." You walk around not wanting to talk, not wanting to smile. That's why you can only be comfortable with other junkies that are "below well" three quarters of the time. Misery loves company!

But when anyone makes that score, it's like Christmas. That's why all the crazy drug addicts and junkies loved me- "the Jewelry dude," the businessman- they loved me. I didn't give a shit. If I had it, I'd share. If somebody was with me, I'd buy them as many bags as I'd bought for me. I kept Doll going in crack. I didn't care. I didn't care about anything. except shoving that needle in my arm, in my leg, in my neck. My life became living in Doll's house for a while. She would go to work and I'd have to start getting heroin and try to get crack for her. Oh, we were blocks away from the Jersey City people. We had them to deal with. Taz was still around and a few other druggies. But Altoona never ever was consistent and you were paying $40 a bag unless you drove to Pittsburgh and got it for $20 a bag. But that's a fucking hard trip every day and a half of your life.

I got a phone number (from one of the Jersey boys) of a big dealer in Jersey City. The Jersey boy didn't have the money. The only way I would take him is if I talked to the dude myself. Well, I take this other junkie down to Jersey City. He hooks me up. And I mean this place is right out of the movies. This place is what you would think of as the "grid", the inner city, "the hood", gangland, a place not even seen by cops or journalists. You're on the last street. The river's right beside you. And there's row houses, every house filled with crack, heroin, pills- "crack alley" they called it. Well, the first time I went, I met this dude that I had talked to on the phone. He seemed OK. And we just bought a little bit -which is about a hundred bags and I got them for $10 a bag. So, I made that trip, met the dude, had his number.

Now, I'm still good with Dave from Precious Metals and Diamonds Company. He found out about me, well, he knew, because I wasn't buying as much jewelry. I told him I was going to a rehab a little while before that and I went. I told him all about it. I think it was one of my twelve-day jaunts. That was all I was allowed to go for that time. Dave the owner had faith in me. He saw me start from a $1,000 buy to $800,000 in six years. Back in those days, when I came out of a rehab, he thought I was cured. So I still had my credit limit of $100,000 and was still "good to go" with him. But I lied to him as you will see.

So I'm getting this brainstorm... why not get up some real money. The dude, when I met him in Jersey City heard about my jewelry.

He said, "You bring as much jewelry as you can. We're going to trade." He said, "Just bring jewelry. I love diamonds. I love all kinds of shit."

This guy had money. You could tell.

So, as I am buying bags here and bags there, I called one of my favorite customers, the doctor's wife, told her I had these big specials on a couple of tennis bracelets. I think I sold $10,000 worth of tennis bracelets to her for four grand. I probably had about $500,000 worth of jewelry left, all at Doll's house and she had her pick during the day. I just left them laying in her damn living room. She was having a ball with them. So I got up $4,000 cash from the doctor's wife and I went to Precious Metals and Diamonds Company that day for a jewelry buy. It was one of the first buys I had made after rehab. Dave was proud of me for going but I was on heroin again. I only stayed clean for a little while like two days then I was gone. I needed months and months and months, that's what it comes down to. For acute addicts who have been addicted for decades, that shit is in your muscles, in your tissues, in your bones, in your mind which means months to come back.

I made a $17,000 buy, left Precious Metals and Diamonds Company, told Doll I was going to Jersey City for the BIG BUY. I was going to bring back enough heroin so I would never have to worry again in my life. I would be FREE. See, that's what all addicts think- THE BUY. You know what? There is never THE BUY. The more you buy, the more you use. "One is too many and a thousand is not enough." It does not work. But in my insanity, my animalistic state, my life is just shredding apart day by day, just coming unglued. I'm living in another world, a universe that is nothing like real life, the real world. I'm with a civilization of people who should not be there, that are in every city, every town. They need help. They're not going to help themselves. But that's where I am, one of them, but I made it. Oh my God.

So I take this beautiful jewelry-big thick herringbone necklaces, big diamonds, earrings and $4,000 cash and head to Jersey City.

I called the dude up, said I was coming down, and told him what I was bringing -like an idiot. I only met him once.

"I'm coming down by myself," I said. I was too damn honest and trusting.

Anyways it was a wretched eight-hour drive as I was going through withdrawal. Well, I get to the address, walk in the house. There are three black guys and a black woman, a young one. So I bring in the jewelry; I have the money. They see the jewelry case. Suddenly three or four guns come pulling out of their pockets - -pointed right at my head.

"Alright, mother fucker, your day ends now," one of them said.

Then they started talking amongst themselves as they're holding the guns to my head.

"Are we killing him and throwing him in the river? Let's do it."

Thinking back, I can't believe I never flinched and stayed so calm.

I said, "People know I'm here. There will be people here quick if I don't make a phone call." And I kept talking. "You guys, you do not want to kill me."

Somehow, I talked my way out of them killing me. I handed them the jewelry. They got all the cash out of my pocket, $4,000. And I still thought the one guy was going to kill my ass. He never took the gun off my head. The other people put their guns down to the side. He kept his up as they took the stuff.

I said, "Just let me go, please. I will get out of here. I will never return."

The girl, as I was walking out of the door, yells "Stop." She was a wild pretty little thing. "Lay down on your stomach flat," she says.

I thought I was dead. Luckily, I was numb; I had no emotion, no soul. I kind of didn't really feel anything. I couldn't even get scared. I couldn't even frighten myself to death. I just did everything on movement.

"Brain, move your hands, move your legs, lay down."

Just in real time, I did what I was told. And the next thing, I hear her walking.

"Crack, crack," -it just sounded like a firecracker.

She shot me in each one of my ass cheeks and started laughing and smiling, saying, "Look what I did. I always wanted to do that. White boy's got two bullet holes in his ass." is exactly what she said. I think it turned her on!

They ran out of the room. Luckily it was only a little .22 pistol. But I'm in pain and laying there.

Now, other people were in this house but they must've known these dudes were going to rob me because they were hidden. There was no one around. They were all upstairs or somewhere. This was a planned setup. But one girl came downstairs, I'll never forget. This girl couldn't have been more than twenty years old. She helped me. Here, the bullets went about an inch and a quarter in each ass cheek. I was bleeding like a son of a bitch.

She said, "What can I do?"

I remembered, in my jacket, I always carried a pen knife.

I said, "Do you have any tequila?"

She got me some. They always have tequila in crack houses, always. That's for when you run out of crack. There's always tequila or cheap wine. She had about a half bottle of tequila. I poured the tequila over the pen knife, lit it, just kept burning it. And didn't that little girl dig those slugs out of my ass. I mean, I screamed and I moaned. Ahh... she got out both of them and shoved toilet paper in each hole. And the only thing we could find was duct tape in my truck. So I had two open wounds filled with toilet paper and covered with amazing duct tape, the cure all. And of course, I made her pour a pile of tequila in my open wounds just before she shoved the toilet paper in. Now just try to imagine that and try to feel me on this one. It hurt worse than anything I ever experienced in my life. She had to dig that knife down and it felt like it went right through me, but I didn't care. I knew if those bullets weren't out of there, I was a dead man. I would've either bled to death or get infected. She did it. I'll never forget her. She pretty well saved my life.

But this story gets better. She wanted crack and I needed heroin. I just got robbed of all my money. I hadn't had heroin in twenty-four hours and it took me seven to eight hours to get there. I was "jonesing" (going through withdrawal) and I was sick. By this time, it's about 12 midnight, after we did everything. So she took me to bars down River Street. You see, in my truck, I always carried one case of silver, sterling silver -necklaces, bracelets, rings, earrings-probably worth five or $6,000. Silver was so cheap compared to gold. So we get this bright idea to take a case of silver, and try to sell it in these bars on River Street. Now, this was back when smoking was still allowed in bars. It's getting late. I'm in Jersey City on River Street, two holes in my ass, carrying a fucking $6,000 case of silver, walking in these smoke-filled bars with this twenty-year-old girl; she must've been twenty-one but who knows. She was going up to people and I was showing the silver but I couldn't sell a damn thing that night. Nobody would buy anything. I was the only white guy there. I didn't care. This was the real deal. Police did not enter these bars.

So here I am robbed and shot in the ass and withdrawal was getting disgustingly terrible as it always does. My ass was killing me. I just wanted bag of dope. That's all I could think of. No sales -the first bar, no sales- the second bar. It's about 1:30, 2:00 in the morning. I'm ready to pass out from the pain and weakness from loss of blood. The backs of my legs were red but luckily it was dark. Finally, we sold a $40 bracelet to this black girl. Aha, now I can get high. Now that's all I thought about was taking that $40 and buying as many bags of heroin as I could. Well, she hooks me up, goes back to the house up on the second floor, comes out with four bags of heroin. And I shared them with her. It's now going on three.

Here's insanity to the fullest extreme. You would think I would put aside a few bucks for gas to get home. I'm in Jersey City on River Street, two holes in my butt and I spent that $40 on four bags of heroin. We shot each other up. Then I took off from Jersey City broke and in pain. I was just a shell of a man. I had no feelings; I had no soul; I had no heart. I was an animal just running on total blind energy. Dark, dark days. Now I get halfway home and my gas tank's on "E". I start going through these little towns. Luckily it was a Nissan, which got about twenty-five miles to a gallon. I didn't have a dime on me. I was starting to come down from those bags of heroin but was OK. But the pain in my butt was so bad I literally had to drive lying sideways on the bucket seats. I'd shift and then lay down, using my left arm to steer and I'd look up over the dashboard. That's how I was driving.

I come through this little town and there's a Sheetz store. I had a box of steaks in the back of my truck in my secret box. Enter Craig Weaver the salesman. I kicked in; I have no clue. It's amazing the resources we can bring out of us when the experiences we're going through are traumatic. I traded a box of steaks, $50 box, about eight steaks, for $15 worth of gas. I was over halfway home. I don't even know if those damn steaks were any good. They were half frozen. I didn't give a shit.

Now mind you, Doll is home waiting for a big shipment of crack and heroin, the mother lode! Jewelry, $4,000 cash, I was coming home loaded for bear. I was going to make it so we would never run out. That's all drug addicts' way of thinking. We want more. We need more. . .bigger. "One is too many and a thousand is not enough" is etched in stone- in my brain now. I can never touch one opioid- NOT ONE. And since I had my awakening ten years ago, I've never touched one.

Once that door is opened, look out. I might go for three freakin' years, but if I touch one Percocet, one Vicodin, one Loricet, and two months later, I think, *Hey, I took one before, I was fine. I'll take two tonight.* No, not true; it will snowball, ladies and gentlemen. You are an addict for life. And I was an addict for so long, I was chronically addicted. My brain was so twisted and tormented. My reality was being high. My life, in my mind, turned totally upside down. The only way I could function or survive was with tons of heroin in my fucking blood. I wanted to die and welcomed death. Please.

I get home in the morning. I'll never forget walking into Doll's bedroom.

"Honey, we have a problem."

I explained the whole night to her. Oh my God, she got so upset. She wasn't mad about me getting hurt! No empathy whatsoever. She was pissed because I came home with nothing. We fought for days.

CHAPTER 10
Everything Must Go:
MONEY AND SUCCESS TURN EVIL

Finally, I decided I'm going to try another rehab. I had five cases of jewelry left, probably about five or $600,000 worth, and I was using that as my only ways and means to get heroin. That was it. I left my real world, my home and my jewelry store. I was "the Jewelry Dude," but not now. I was going to go to a rehab again, Cove Forge.

Here's how insane I was. I was thinking, *This is it-this is the one*, yet I wasn't ready for a rehab. A rehab was not going to do it. I was close to death. We bought a bunch of crack from the Altoona street natives and smoked rock after rock on the way to Cove Forge. As Doll's driving me, we would stop, pull off the road and take a hit, then pull off the road again and take another hit. I walked into Cove Forge with my heart racing quadruple what it should be. Doll just took off and went home with the bunch of rocks I left her with. I traded about $2,000 worth of jewelry for maybe $200 worth of rocks. I had lost all sense of value, judgement, business. The diamonds, gold necklaces that took me years to amass, now meant nothing to me. My world was spinning out of control and death sounded like a great idea.

The problem with rehabs is they give very little to knock you out. The last thing they want to do is fill you with drugs. After all, you are an addict. You can get addicted to anything. You might get a minor barbiturate to help you sleep but in Cove Forge you are raw. It's a tough tough kick out. I'll never forget the second day in there and I'm really trying. They're coming in taking my blood pressure every couple hours.

I'm sick and hurting. That urge was coming on so fucking strong. I needed a bag of dope. I was climbing the walls -lying down for a while, getting up, lying down, getting up.

I met a guy in there, a pretty cool dude who was in there for crack addiction. We shared a room together. That was a mistake. He was from Harrisburg, Pennsylvania and was very well connected with all the damn dealers. So about the fourth day with hundreds of thousands worth of jewelry out there, (I could trade it in at any jewelry store for one tenth the amount, -or trade it to the dealers or junkies for drugs), I talked him into leaving with me.

I called Doll. "I'm healed! I'm better."

I know what she was thinking... "Come home."

"Well, Doll, I met a friend..."

And as soon as I mention crack, cocaine, Doll was out to get me and my buddy. I bring this guy home to Doll's house. It was totally insane, twisted, sick. And it gets worse. Dad and I had a Mercedes Benz that we both paid half for. It was a used but nice car and we only paid $15,000 for it. He had it over at his house, couldn't trust me with it. I had a key though. It was half mine. Now, thinking what I did, I still to this day can't believe I did it. Dad and Diane were away on a four-day trip. So I went over, grabbed the Mercedes Benz and brought it over to Doll's house.

This guy I just met; I'll never forget what I said to him, "You take my Mercedes Benz and you go to Harrisburg and come back with as much shit as you can get."

And I'm running in and out of Doll's house bringing out diamonds, rings, bracelets, gold necklaces. I'm even throwing the gold necklaces over his freakin' neck. I had traded a bunch in at a jewelry store and got about $800 for $20,000 worth of jewelry. So I give this lunatic all this jewelry, beautiful gold and diamonds, and about $1,000 cash.

"Go, young man. Go and come back with gifts. You must hurry."

The son of a bitch takes off and I can remember when he was leaving, he was begging me to go with him.

"Craig," he said, "What are you doing?!"

He knew he couldn't handle this mission. How insane is this?

He had more sense than I did. I couldn't go. I weighed about 120 pounds. I was dying. Every time I'd take a drink of alcohol, I'd "puke" my guts out and I was hurting all over from the track mark sores and scars.

I said, "Go. Get going."

Well, one day passes, two days pass, three days pass. He quit calling me. No communication at all.

Dad gets home. "Where the hell's the Mercedes Benz?"

I make up some insane story. "Oh, it's fine. It's over here Dad. No problem."

Dad was afraid even to come around me back then. He and Diane were hitting it off great and were in their first couple years of being together. They were in love. He didn't want anything to do with me.

The kid never come back. The car was gone. Well, the stupid crazy shit we do. We are the definition of insanity when we're addicted- repeating the same thing over and over again trying to get different results. Bullshit.

About a week later, Dad calls me, "Got a call from the state police down in Harrisburg. They found our Mercedes in a back alley dented; windows busted out."

Luckily Dad had the best insurance on it. He got it back, got it fixed up and sold it for about twelve grand. I wanted nothing to do with the money, nothing to do with him, and nothing to do with the car. This is just one of the stories that happened on a regular basis.

Now I had lost all sense of reality and my time was growing short. I was literally dying. I wasn't eating. But I'd find some way every day to score bags of heroin and crack. After all, I was "The Jewelry Dude." That shit was coming out of me faster than it was going into me. I couldn't get high anymore. My endorphins were a mess. I didn't know if I was high or if I was normal.

Doll and I became friends with about three or four of the Jersey City Boys in Altoona and they started coming over and having crack and heroin parties with us. Those were days that I wished I could end my life and commit suicide. I started thinking about it all the time. My whole life was nothing but drugs, drugs, drugs. I'd run around with these nuts all day. Suicide was becoming a priority. I knew I couldn't go on much longer.

I had made it. I had made it into the world of the junkyard dogs, the world where nothing matters. Your eyes are sunk in and hollow. Your mind is twisted while your body aches, scars everywhere. Daylight sucked. You hated walking out during the day, but you had to every day get your daily quota. Doll was almost losing her job being late all the time, missing days of work. I knew it couldn't go on but you don't think like that. In fact, you don't think. You just do. I was lying, I was cheating, I was stealing. No more communications with Dad or my kids. I couldn't even sell food, ladies and gentlemen. I couldn't go to my customers. I disappeared as I so did many times. But this time I was truly gone.

One night, I went to Taz's house. He had just got some heroin in and I had enough money for one or two bags. Remember now, Taz charged $40 a bag. But I took three cases of my jewelry with me just in case anyone there would want to trade. Well, it was a setup. I'm upstairs on the third floor for about an hour, shot a couple of bags. I think I traded a $10,000 tennis bracelet for about five bags of heroin. That was good business!? I go back out to my truck. It was broken into. All three jewelry cases were gone! I went home to Doll's house. She wasn't there. I had had it. I was in a rage.

Oddly there was one thought that entered my mind when I looked behind the seats in my truck that night. I swear to God, I said to myself, "Good, thank God, I'm almost there."

You know what that meant. I knew subconsciously I was dying and I was a dead man unless I got rid of all monetary things.

People, I would drive down the road for weeks and no matter where I was going, I would envision buildings falling in front of me, skyscrapers, just like an earthquake, just crumbling in front of me.

And I would think to myself, *Everything must go. I must get rid of everything to save myself.* I would see this every time I drove around- every time. I actually could not wait to be penniless. I was alone in my cruel world of desperation and madness.

Well, that night, I went home to Doll's house and took the remaining jewelry. Doll was probably partying with another guy or out somewhere where she could get crack. She was an addict. I was gone. I wasn't much use to her anymore. I couldn't do much of anything except try to find a fucking vein and I couldn't even do that. I took the last couple cases and drove down to the little Juniata River near Lewistown where it's super deep. And I threw that jewelry right in the river. I just tossed it. I came home about three or four in the morning. Doll was there.

I said, "It's done. It's gone."

She said, "What did you do?" I told her I was robbed. "They took about $300,000 worth of jewelry, stole it from me. It was just a bunch of the fucking street gang, Taz's friends, my buddies, my junkyard dog friends. They knew where I kept it in the back seat behind the seats. They knew I'd go to Taz's house all the time. It was a setup."

She said, "What did you do with the rest?" Her eyes got really big when I told her. It's four in the morning and Doll kicks me out of her house.

"Get the hell out of here!" she cried, "You're disgusting."

Well, I was no good to her anymore. I had nothing- zero, no jewelry, no money.

CHAPTER 11
TOTAL INSANITY: DEATH SOUNDS DAMN GOOD

I was a broken man. I had reached my destination, ladies and gentlemen. I arrived. I was lower than low. But you know what, somewhere deep inside I had a little burning ember. I could not commit suicide yet. I could not kill myself. I went over to Taz's. He let me crash on the third floor just for that night but I couldn't stay there. There was a guy whose parents were rich. He was the biggest junkie out of the junkies that I was running with. His parents wanted rid of him so bad they bought him a trailer on the back road to Bellwood.

They just paid for it and said, "This is yours. Get out of our house." He was about twenty-six. I can't mention his name. He comes from a very well to do family in Altoona.

I'm chain smoking as I'm going through this. My heart is heavy. This is hard, so hard to go back. But please, everyone that is reading this, just know, just know one thing, addiction is deadly. It's no joke. It will sap all that is good out of you. Forget about love. Forget about happiness. Forget about enjoying your life. You can throw away everything you worked for right out the fucking window. People will learn to hate you especially the people closest to you because those are the ones you take advantage of. We hurt the ones we love because they love us. They are targets. You can bullshit them the most. Tough story. Tough life.

But there's one thing that I should've never had- my checkbook. I had my checkbook in the glove compartment. So I hook up with this addict who lived in the trailer on the backroad to Bellwood.

He's ecstatic. "I have "the Jewelry Dude" to myself." Well, it's about November or December. It was cold, it was winter.

"Come with me to my trailer and you can stay here as long as you want." There were two couches in the living room. It was a nice double wide but he paid no bills. There was no TV, no electricity, no heat. I slept on one couch and he slept on the other. I froze to death; it was freezing in that place.

This part is going to be very hard. All I had left was a checkbook but up in Clearfield, Philipsburg, State College, I sold to all the bank employees. Even though they hadn't seen me for a while, they all thought I was a great successful businessman. They were with me for years and years and years. Somehow, I hid my addiction from them. The further away from Altoona, the less they knew. So we jump in my truck and head to Clearfield. I'm going to try this once. I went into the Clearfield Bank and got up enough zest and energy to use my salesmanship. I wrote an $800 check, walked in, handed it to the girl and talked to her, told her I was in a hurry. She never even checked my account and gave me the money.

Now there was a place in Altoona, I'll never forget. It was a house with a husband and wife and about three or four kids running around. Even in the shape I was in, I couldn't believe what I was seeing. We walked into this house. The kids were all naked. The parents were heroin addicts. Garbage was piled up in every room about two to three feet. No toilet paper in the house and the kids were screaming about that. These people were so twisted, they would put ten to fifteen bags of heroin into a ladle, a ladle that you dip in soup that you get a bowlful of. And they would shoot that up. I got sick in the house. But they had heroin. They always had heroin. This was my last remaining place to get my drugs. I had burned all my bridges, gotten rid of all my jewelry.

But I had $800 in my pocket. Now, we bought a ton of heroin, as much as we could get, about $40 a bag. I think they might've taken it down to $35. I'm pretty sure they did. There's a graveyard on Route 36 that had iron gates in front of it. Back in the early 1900s, it was built. We got our dope and drove up into this graveyard about 10 in the morning and we sat there. In the back of the graveyard, nobody could see us shooting heroin. He passed out after about the third or fourth shot. I sat there all day staring at the tombstones. Why? Why was I so comfortable there? Why did I think I needed to be there? That was my safety zone, my safe place. We shot up until the heroin was gone, $800 worth. He would come to, shoot up a bag, pass out, come to, shoot up another bag, pass out. Not me. That shit was coming out of me faster than it was going in.

But I couldn't pass out; I couldn't "nod." That's the big term for all heroin junkies. When you "nod," that's coming in and out of consciousness, that's the high point. That's where everybody tries to get.

"I 'nodded' for six hrs."

"Oh, you were in dreamland. You are great, man."

So sick!

We go back to his trailer at night, wake up the next morning, and this time we go to Philipsburg. We did the same thing with a $700 check. Then we go back again to this nightmare of a home and watch them shooting up from their ladle. But I wouldn't partake. I couldn't believe it. This was after I saw them searching for a needle underneath their couch and using that. Once you're a heroin addict and a junkie, you share needles. You don't care where they come from, who shoots them. I had hepatitis C by then.

Back to the graveyard…I wanted to die so bad. I did not want any more of this world. When I could get in front of a TV, I'd watch all of the ghost shows, the ghost adventures, all the paranormal shows I could find, to make sure there was life after death. Isn't that sad? I wanted to know that when I died which was going to be shortly, that I'd still go on. I was researching my death. This went on for about two weeks. Finally, the checks started catching up, through the mail, back through the banks. I started getting turned down. "Well, your check bounced."

"Oh my God, what the hell! There's gotta be a mistake."

"Your check bounced Craig. Another bank."

One day it was snowing out. I woke up about eight in the morning and didn't want to move. I was ready to commit suicide. I still wasn't sure how I was going to do it. But I was going to do it. Do you think I hit bottom yet? ladies and gentlemen. These fucking "bottoms" are deep, man and they hurt.

Suddenly there was a knock at the door. I couldn't even get up. It was the second day without any heroin. I just lay there. I think I grunted. I heard my dad's voice.

"Craig, are you in there?"

"Help!" That door broke in so quick. My dad drug me out of there, half carried me. I'm slumped over the seat in the car. We didn't talk. We didn't say a word. Just to look at me was enough-white pale skin, wounds-big welts everywhere from "missing"-trying to shoot up, same clothes I had on for weeks. I don't know when I showered last. It hurt to shower, water hitting all these nasty sores and wounds. And there was no electricity in his trailer.

My dad drove right to White Deer Run, Williamsport, Pa., a two-hour drive. I had been there once for twelve days when I was with Nancy. But twelve days wasn't enough. I can remember they took one look at me and I was in a bed in a matter of thirty to forty min., who knows. I didn't move for three days. Thank God, it was a methadone rehab. About the third day, I got my methadone, 30mg. It makes you normal. You don't get high but you feel normal.

I'll never forget, once that hit me, and I felt normal and could think again, realizing, *Oh my God, what have I done?! Everything's gone!* I subconsciously got rid of everything. There was nowhere for me to go, nothing I could do.

But you know what, ladies and gentlemen, thank God I had nowhere to go, no means of getting any money, no means of buying any dope. I was a broken man. That was my "bottom". I had had it.

My father, despite all the problems we had during our youth, saved my life. He was the only one that cared. He became a detective and went down into the depths of hell, the backstreets of Altoona, talking to anyone he could find.

He had hunted me down.

Isn't it funny how things happen? He was the one that I used to blame for a lot of my problems. But he was the only one who cared. You see, I now know it takes two. My father and my mother both had issues with each other. They should've never been married. But they stayed married for the kids back then, in the fifties and sixties. Mom would push his buttons and she didn't drink. She was sly and conniving and Dad was just a young beer drinking railroader. And we kids got thrown in the middle of it. I guess, shit happens.

The one thing I really really want to get across is to all parents out there, when you're young, when you have kids, I don't care how old they are- four, five, six, seven, eight -they see and hear everything. And they don't forget it, especially traumatic things, especially things that jolt them, things that hurt them, things that cause them to be in fear or panic or cry. They don't forget and those things linger and fester and build inside of them. I know. I went through it.

So really, it's just the perfect storm that caused all this and now I'm waking up in White Deer Run. And I have nowhere to turn and that is a freakin' good thing. Now this time I was ready for White Deer Run. I was ready for a rehab. I was ready for a new life. There comes a point when you have gone through so much pain and misery, it affects you in such a way that you have no self-esteem left, you have no sense of being left. You have no pride. You have nothing positive. You feel like a piece of shit.

You see, all those years, I was so busy amassing my fortune. To this day, I don't know anyone who worked as hard as I did. All the logistics involved, all the houses I went to everyday delivering food and jewelry, all those towns, I got to know everybody in, was unbelievable. Hell, there were times when I came home from Oakland, Maryland, Deep Creek Lake with $10,000 in my pocket. That's just from one day's work- usually at least $3,000 in food which I'd unload within three to four hours and $500 checks, $600 checks or more because they'd always grab jewelry from me. The two combined so well.

But everything I did back in those days, because I was addicted to opioids, and had a disease, I always felt less than; I always felt I didn't deserve this. It takes away all your humanity and when I made a decision to get rid of everything, I actually did not make that consciously. I was sabotaging my businesses subconsciously without even realizing it. I knew deep down inside, to save my life, to save Craig Weaver, I must start totally over again.

So here I am in my early 60's and it hurts today. It hurts so bad. I remember driving 400 miles a day, being at peoples' houses at exact precise times, and lugging big cases of food and jewelry through rain and snow. I'd leave a house selling $1,000, $2,000, $6,000 but because of my addiction, I didn't deserve it.

Looking back, I have been with so many women, so many beautiful women. But I couldn't keep any of them. I wanted instant gratification. That's all I knew how to do. The first thing I would do with women I just met was seduce them. I was good at it. Being very savvy, loving and charming was easy. I had no problem seducing women and never took the time to get to know them as friends.

And yes, I've been married a few times. After the sex wears out which it always does, we had nothing else to do, nothing else in common. So many beautiful women have crossed my path and I screwed it up every single time.

So White Deer Run saved my life! After thirty days I was to leave because that's all the insurance paid for. But they would not let me go! Thank the Lord, they kept me and this time I finally stayed long enough to feel human again, and to have at least a final shot of some assemblance of a life.

So it was fifty-four days at White Deer Run. I had lost so many battles over decades but this disease did not kill me.

Now it's my turn. Get ready, the BEST is yet to come!

CHAPTER 12
BACK FROM HELL: A NEW LIFE

White Deer Run saved my life. I actually stayed long enough to get my head straightened out, but it was not near anything normal, as that would take years! It did take away the animalistic drive to kill myself and get off the planet. I walked out of White Deer Run with absolutely nothing left in the world. I was a broken man.

Here's what still confuses me today. It's hard to put into words. I think about the decades of hard work building a food and jewelry empire with thousands of customers. But in my mind, I did not deserve any of that success. I swear to you I was not able to get clean and stay clean until every last penny I earned was gone! Why?

Why didn't Dad grab those jewelry cases?

Why couldn't I stash it away somewhere?

I can remember times of making three and four grand profits in a day. But it did nothing for me. It was like any other day. Why? I think my own self guilt of being an addict and low self-esteem was making me suffer as if I didn't suffer enough. Money came too easy for me and I had no idea how to control it. I always wanted everyone around me to be happy and enjoy themselves and we all did. There is so much deeper going on. OK I'm thinking way deep. It must be my constitution and DNA makeup.

Just the other day, I said to my dad, "Why does everything going on in this country hit me so hard? I'm this small peon. These things are way out of my control." But I get hit so hard when I see the ripping apart of our constitution, our country.

Going back to my addiction, something inbred throughout my genetic structure is and has always affected me my whole life. Even though I made 99% of my money legally, "I did not deserve it." I am now sixty-three and clean except for a minute amount of methadone. My mind is still amazing me as my thoughts are so clear. I can figure things out and analyze them down to their origin. There are times when complex situations become so simple, so crisp and clear.

One past mind set has served me well. Make believe you are the main character in your movie (which you are). Every situation you encounter, do what the main character would do. Stay on point, be the hero! I have a lust for life and a curiosity about everything. I am literally an encyclopedia on opioid addiction and have sent many, many people to rehab. I do not touch even alcohol and am getting high on life. It is a huge adventure taking every day and doing what I can do. I have missed so, so much.

My kids have not grasped everything yet. Lisle turned out to be a lawyer and journalist. Kelcie is a physician's assistant. I love them to death and am so proud of everything they have become. That is my next challenge, to be back in their lives. I left them on purpose so as not to spread amazing dysfunctionality towards them. I am sad. I hurt every day. I lived through massive childhood dysfunctionality and believe you me, it was a crazy life.

Obsessive compulsive disorder is the main factor in all addicts. Other things play a role but people without bad OCD can take opiates and stop. They can have a sexual relationship and not destroy it by obsessing and wearing it out.

Any kind of addiction is a byproduct of OCD. I think all humans have a little OCD but most are controllable. But there are those of us that are haunted constantly by a relentless stream of bad or negative experiences. They pulsate through our minds constantly with no escape or rest. We are hammered every minute of the day.

Once we find our drug of choice, it becomes our salvation. It whisks us away from the never-ending torment we fight constantly. This becomes the largest human conundrum for all drug addicts. The exact thing that saves us from our hell on earth is slowly killing us creating another worse hell on earth.

So our tormented souls while being rescued by chemical intervention are also being captured by a deeper darker demon that walks us down into never ending caverns and tunnels. We are led to the darkest of dark worlds. No light. No escape. And all alone. We are introduced to pure evil. Pure hell on earth. This is a road all addicts will travel. No one knows our pain and suffering.

It took me awhile to get back to society. It was a slow and tedious process taking at least three years to become centered mentally. After the rehab, I was arrested for all the bad checks I wrote during my descent into hell. I still had customers way out on the fringes that did not know my plight. I went to AA and NA for a while. It's not for everyone. The social system was too crazy for my fragile mind. The women are looking for men and vice versa. Next thing, the games start. The danger is our way of thinking. We must not go back into our addictive personalities. Becoming a player is too dangerous.

I fell in love two years into being clean. NO! Come on, I did not know what love was. I fell into lust. She was beautiful but bad for me. She drank and partied. Even though I never touched an opiate, I started drinking. For a couple of years, I drank with her. Of course, things went south. I was not growing mentally and spiritually. Then her sons moved in. Both were into heroin and opiates.

Finally, I told her, "Either them or me." Well, I was gone and never went back.

Now I am on the right path and have a passion that grows every day. I'm making enough money to pay the bills. I picked up painting and some carpentry. Now I'm happy but I'm not. I am writing this book and beginning a new life of motivational speaking and helping other sick and suffering addicts.

I am sixty-three years old but mentally my mind is still waking up. I am still growing and getting so creative, like starting over at age nineteen. Mentally, I'm a grateful man. No matter what problems arise on a daily basis, I am so much happier. I'm FREE! I'm not in HELL ON EARTH. I love life but I'm not done living.

Right now, we have the Covid pandemic hitting our lives full force. Now I think it's been handled wrong. The lockdowns and masks are taking their toll mentally. There is some type of revolution going on. It's now August 2021 and already over 90,000 Americans have died from opioids this year.

A big new wave of evil - deadly Fentanyl - 50-100 times more potent than morphine - is overtaking the world. We are being attacked from many fronts. People, mainly our youth, need educated about the dangers of opioid addiction. At this critical time, I am starting an opioid crisis movement.

CRAIG WEAVER'S OPIOID CRISIS MOVEMENT!

God bless the addicts who have read this book and God bless all of us!

Hopefully you will hear from me again.